Charles
SPURGEON

THE PRINCE OF PREACHERS

D0980378

J. C. CARLILE

Abridged and edited by
DAN HARMON

BARBOUR
PUBLISHING

All scripture quotations, unless otherwise noted, are taken from the King James Version of the Bible.

Cover illustration © Dick Bobnick
Cover design by Douglas Miller (mhpubarts.com)

Published by Barbour Publishing, Inc., P.O. Box 719, Uhrichsville, Ohio 44683, www.barbourbooks.com

Our mission is to publish and distribute inspirational products offering exceptional value and biblical encouragement to the masses.

Member of the
Evangelical Christian
Publishers Association

Printed in the United States of America.
5 4 3 2 1

FOREWORD

Charles H. Spurgeon was undoubtedly a man for his time. What would he do in these days? We do not know. But if he were here, God would no doubt find him ready to respond to His will, regardless of the demand.

Those who knew Spurgeon personally bear a wonderful testimony to his life, character, and work. Spurgeon not only influenced those around him but also seemed to fashion them after his own model. They were, at least in spirit, all similar, all following their pastor, leader, and friend. Their characteristics were faithfulness to the Truth, love for the souls of men and women, independence in thought and action, and a deep love for the Savior. The spirit of Spurgeon long hovered over all the spheres of his work in London— at the New Park Street Tabernacle, orphanage, college, colportage, and almshouses.

Spurgeon was a powerful witness to and expositor of the Bible. His contributions to evangelical thought can never be obliterated. The doctrines of grace were his meat and drink. The Savior was a living personality to him constantly.

Spurgeon was a theologian of the first order and, as a preacher, a master of homiletics. His literary knowledge was extensive. He possessed a great mind. Through declining titles, he was able to touch all classes and conditions of humanity. Leading politicians, scientists, military officers, students, and clergymen of all denominations were among his audiences. He was fully convinced of the truths he taught and always could give scriptural reasons for his beliefs. The Bible was his message, armory, confidence, and argument. He preached the eternal election of humans to everlasting life, but he equally stressed human accountability to God. He never hesitated to proclaim truths he could not fully reconcile in his own mind, if they were in God's Word.

Grace was one of Spurgeon's favorite topics. His kindheartedness and generosity were what most impressed many of those who knew him, and he instilled these characteristics in others. Numerous ministers and missionaries were started on their careers by financial assistance from Spurgeon.

The Holy Spirit made him a great soul winner. Many people abroad attributed their conversions to Spurgeon's ministry. Truly, God made His minister a flame of fire.

Spurgeon was not only a great preacher but a pastor whose spiritual influence was great among his flock. When asked why he was so phenomenally successful, he frequently would reply, "My people pray for me." And what prayer meetings they had in those days! Hundreds gathered on Monday evenings at his church. Those and smaller prayer groups continued long after his death.

Indeed, Spurgeon was never out of touch with his Lord. A friend recalled a train trip with Spurgeon and several others when, in the midst of their jovial conversation, Spurgeon suddenly said, "Brethren, I have just remembered something. Let us pray about it together." He related the need and, for the next few minutes, led them in prayer. At a deacons meeting, a great need in one of the branches of the ministry was being discussed. Prayer was suggested. But Spurgeon interrupted, took a sheet of paper, wrote "C. H. Spurgeon, fifty pounds," and passed it around for the others to add their names and amounts. "Now, brethren," he said, "we can conscientiously pray."

Such was the man who was empowered to do a work which even today points to God's faithfulness and the power of His Gospel, reaching the uttermost parts of the earth.

PREFACE

Born and raised in England, Charles Haddon Spurgeon was one of the most influential Baptist ministers of his day. During his lifetime, he introduced thousands of people from all walks of life to the Lord through his preaching. Although he had little formal education, Spurgeon's life and works impacted lives on both sides of the Atlantic.

Spurgeon's inspiring story of faith and commitment will challenge you to seek a deeper relationship with Jesus Christ.

ONE

Londoners love pageants. They turn out from every direction for a great occasion. Coronations and other celebrations attract hundreds of thousands of spectators, but London's greatest crowds gather for funerals in the time-honored English tradition of paying homage to the departed. When Wellington's body was carried through the streets, there was hardly standing space along the route.

February 8, 1892, saw London honor a man without a title or even an academic degree. He had no political reputation, no aristocratic connections. The funeral procession, more than two miles long, included men and women of all social classes and economic conditions. The simple olive casket at the head was carried amid palm branches and flowers. Newspapers reported that more than one hundred thousand people participated in the memorial services, and practically all London suspended activities in respect for the deceased.

"What are they waiting for?" asked a stranger, looking at

the packed thousands standing at the entrance to Norwood Cemetery.

"Don't you know? It's Spurgeon's funeral," said a woman in a whisper.

"Spurgeon? You mean the preacher at the tabernacle? Well, I never thought London cared so much about any preacher."

At the close of a sermon on December 27, 1874, C. H. Spurgeon had remarked with uncanny insight:

> In a little while there will be a concourse of persons in the streets. Methinks I hear someone inquiring, "What are all these people waiting for?"
>
> "Do you not know he is to be buried today?"
>
> "And who is that?"
>
> "It is Spurgeon."
>
> "What? The man that preached at the tabernacle?"
>
> "Yes, he is to be buried today."
>
> That will happen very soon, and when you see my coffin carried to the silent grave, I would like every one of you, whether converted or not, to be constrained to say, "He did earnestly urge us in plain and simple language not to put off consideration of eternal things. He did entreat us to look at Christ. Now he is gone. Our blood is not at his door if we perish."

Spurgeon was far-seeing, with the gift of seeing the unseen. Often he literally told people things about themselves which they alone knew. He would give sufficient indication to let the person know he was speaking of him or her, then add some detail that filled the individual with fear or contrition.

But he was much more than a seer. Spurgeon was among the elect, one of the great souls transcending all the barriers of parties and sects and even nationalities. He belonged to the world and to all time.

He made life glad and sweet. Many homes were called by his Christian name: Haddon Hall, Haddon Villa, Haddon Cottage. His likeness was displayed in countless homes. It is difficult to estimate Spurgeon's influence. Dr. A. T. Pierson made an interesting calculation:

> *I find that Mr. Spurgeon must have preached to no less than ten million people. During his pastorate he must have received into the communion of the Church between ten and twelve thousand converts. His sermons must have reached a total of between twenty and forty million readers, and it is probable that today there are more than fifty million people reading of Christ whom he loved, and of his labors in the past. His sermons have gone round the world, translated into twenty-three tongues and dialects we know of: French, Italian, Spanish, German, Dutch, Swedish, Russian, Chinese, Japanese, Syriac, Arabic, South American tongues, those of the islands of the South Seas, of the continents of Asia, of Africa and of Europe, into every part of the earth they have gone, and it is impossible to form a correct or exact estimate of the marvelous influence of that one voice and of that one pen.*

At the end of his life, all Europe seemed anxious to hear the latest news while the great preacher lay sick in Menton in the south of France. Inquiries came from the highest and lowest in the land. All the press made arrangements for special reports, and when the pilgrim came to the end of the journey, even Fleet Street stood in salute.

The English newspapers vied with each other in their tributes to "the greatest and the last of the Puritans." The *Times* devoted columns to estimating Spurgeon's influence and analyzing his qualities. Dr. Robertson Nicoll wrote:

> *With all these he combines the manliness of a genuine Englishman. There is nothing weak or morbid about his mind; indeed, if he has a defect it is that there is too little pathos in his sermons. He is, if we may be allowed the expression, a typical John Bull, and it is his John Bullism in religion that has made him so popular with all classes of the community. All know him to be every inch a man, and even those most hostile to his opinions are proud of him. The charity child who, on being asked who was the Prime Minister of England, replied, "Spurgeon," was not far from the truth.*

John Bull was a nickname invented by a political writer in the early 1700s. The name has been used to describe and caricature a typical Englishman. John Bull is rather proud of himself and his name. He has been derided by novelists and self-appointed critics.

No doubt there was some justification for the ugly portraits, but there is another type of John Bull. Perhaps it is not too much to say C. H. Spurgeon represented the characteristics of the real John Bull consecrated to the service of Jesus Christ.

John Bullism in Spurgeon was a downrightness that makes one entirely dependable. His "yea" was "yea" and his "nay" was "nay." He did not compromise in matters of religion. Some of his sternest words condemned playing fast and loose with the truth. He had sympathy and compassion for the thief, the harlot, and the drunkard, but for the distorter of truth he had the whip. John Bullism in Spurgeon was a love of reality, an attempt to clear the air.

There is a love of adventure in John Bull. He is a seagoing man, a pioneer who loves sailing the uncharted ocean and trying the unknown path. Likewise, Spurgeon's religion was not a conservative, dull affair confined to Sundays and churches. There was something of romance about it. It was a conflict, a going forth to war—and Spurgeon loved the battlefield. Moral sedatives were not for him. He felt the call of the blood, the response of chivalry.

John Bull perhaps takes himself too seriously and is too self-confident. The John Bull in Spurgeon was not conceited, although if anyone might have been forgiven for having a good opinion of himself, it was Spurgeon. No building in London was large enough to contain the crowds who wanted to hear his voice. No church in the world had a roll call of more than half the membership of Spurgeon's.

Another characteristic of John Bull is a rough exterior that disregards the opinions of others. Yet Spurgeon once wrote:

I was reading an article in a newspaper, very much in my praise. It always makes me feel sad, so sad that I could cry, if ever I see anything praising me; it breaks my heart. I feel I do not deserve it, and then I say: Now I must try to do better, so that I may deserve it. If the world abuses me I am a match for that, I begin to like it. It may fire all its big guns at me; I will not return a solitary shot but just store them up and grow rich upon the old iron.

All through his preaching, Spurgeon related the gospel of Christ to questions of conduct. His standard was Christlikeness. It was the one test of reality. In this, his John Bullism was very assertive. There were no halftones. The saved people lived the saved life. "By their fruits ye shall know them." His foundations were grim but stern and enduring, putting all the weight on the character and purpose of God as revealed in Jesus Christ.

Christian World in February 1892 stated:

> *Any attempt to estimate Spurgeon's place in the religious life of England must take note of the outstanding fact that he touched the lives of great multitudes and quickened them to finer issues. No human computation will be able to reckon the number of weary toilers in the working- and lower-middle classes whose narrow surroundings have been brightened and idealised by the glow from the realm of faith to which he introduced them. It was a great thing which this man achieved, to convince multitudes of struggling people in the midst of a life which everything tended to belittle, that their character and career were a matter of infinite concern to the Power who made them; that they could not afford to treat sin lightly or to throw themselves away as though they were of no account.*

Spurgeon was supreme in the pulpit. Calling "a spade a spade," he struck a new note in preaching. Natural but not vulgar, he was blunt, sometimes almost brutal, with his words. With skilled art and absolute honesty, he described things as they were.

Spurgeon frequently used illustrations drawn from

common incidents. Other teachers quoted classic stories. He told the simple tale so familiar that anyone with a seeing eye and understanding heart could relate to it. The activities of the world always interested him. He was far more concerned with people than places. He had the gift of seeing all that was there. He could draw word pictures with geometrical accuracy. All the details of the story were true to life, reproductions of actuality, trifles that added up to perfection.

Great preachers like Spurgeon speak to the universal humanity. They touch on chords familiar to everyone. They hold up no vague, beautiful ideal, but the truth that all can recognize.

Spurgeon was influenced in his artistic speech by the Authorized Version of the English Bible and the authors Shakespeare and John Bunyan. His sermons were rich in classical quotations and allusions. He did not use Latin phrases or polysyllabic sentences like other preachers of his time. He spoke sweet, simple English, clear in its meaning, strong and unyielding, yet tender and refreshing as a welcome summer breeze.

His thought and speech were inseparable, sincere and straightforward. He loved words. He delighted in dissecting them, turning them about to see just where they fit. Some of his spoken messages seemed to lose effect when printed—he diligently revised his own work and insisted on finding the right term to express his meaning.

Great changes have taken place in the social and religious life of England since Spurgeon's death. In his time, he was almost without competition. Electronic media was unknown, automobiles an as-yet-unrealized reality. There were relatively few distractions from churchgoing. And in the pulpit, Spurgeon was the greatest preacher—perhaps of any time or land. The Metropolitan Tabernacle where he preached became something of a nonconformist shrine, the home of the largest congregation in London.

Ministers all over the world were trained in Spurgeon's college, proclaiming the things for which he stood. Dr. Fullerton wrote in *Souls of Men*:

> *We may be inclined to say that Spurgeon's Tabernacle, Spurgeon's College, and Spurgeon's Orphanage are his legacy, but it would be nearer the mark to say that they are only his memorial. We can rejoice in the fine tribute their prosperity pays to his memory, but they can scarcely be looked upon as his chief contribution to the life of today. A similar verdict might be given as regards the amazing library that he has left us. I write facing what is perhaps the finest collection of his works: one hundred and three volumes bound in calf; and the more I consult them the greater is the wonder that one brain and one pen could be responsible for them all. But they are not his legacy, they are not available to most people, and their very prodigality makes it difficult to find the way through them, but selections of them are still used and valued. The most unexpected people sometimes testify that they read a Spurgeon sermon in preparation for Sunday, or actually read one before resting every night. I ask myself, what is it they are seeking? Whatever it is, it is his legacy.*

Now what is Spurgeon's legacy? At length, on awaking one morning, it came to me as if spoken by the very voice of God: "His testimony is to the converting power of the gospel." The conversion of his hearers was the constant aim of his ministry, and therefore the constant result of it. The word "therefore" is not used thoughtlessly. His often-quoted rejoinder to his first student came from his own experience. When Medhurst complained that he was not having conversions, Spurgeon said in assumed surprise: "But you do not expect conversions every time you preach, do you?" "Oh, no, of course not!" "And that is why you do not have them!"

Fullerton's opinion is worthy of all respect, but we cannot accept it in explaining Spurgeon's legacy. Testimony to the converting power of the gospel has been given for nearly two thousand years. The apostle Paul recorded that he was not ashamed of the gospel of Christ. Whitefield, Wesley, Moody, Fullerton himself, and countless other preachers have attested to the converting power of the gospel. They all have learned by experience that He is able to save to the utmost.

We must go deeper to find Spurgeon's secret. He was a colossal man of many sides. He certainly was an expert in dealing with the souls of men. No man of the Victorian age invaded the spheres of life with such penetrating, far-reaching influence as did Spurgeon. He was a massive personality, a granite boulder torn from the rugged hillside, a landmark in the history of the church, a rare man of destiny. He was truly the last of the great Puritans, towering above others of his time like a great Alpine mountain, an attraction to storms, a solitary figure bearing the loneliness that is the price of leadership. He had no successor; such leaders leave followers but not successors.

What was it that made the son of an obscure country minister the greatest orator of modern times, the greatest evangelist since Paul? There have been many answers but no explanation.

Spurgeon once said, "When I am gone, all sorts of people will write [about] my life. They will have some difficulty in accounting for the position God has given me. I can tell you two reasons why I am what I am." He paused. "My mother, and the truth of my message."

His mother and his message accounted for much. Was there ever a great man without a great woman near— frequently his mother? Spurgeon owed much to the gracious, simple woman who told him at her knee the old, old story that he clothed in new forms with wondrous power.

And Spurgeon undoubtedly believed wholeheartedly in the truth of his message. He was impatient with those who qualified or modified the gospel. He literally believed the grace of God is powerful enough to change lives and save eternally. His Savior was no dead Christ buried under the Syrian sky, but the Lord who lives forever, mighty to save.

Yet mother and message are insufficient to account for the wonderful personality that took London by storm. His brother, Dr. James A. Spurgeon, copastor at the Tabernacle for many years, had the same mother and the same message, but was a very different type of man. We do not compare the brothers; they were colleagues and worked harmoniously, supplementing each other's gifts. But they were as unlike as any two men could be.

An American minister introduced to C. H. Spurgeon, told him, "I have long wished to see you, Mr. Spurgeon, and to put one or two simple questions to you. Would you mind answering?"

Spurgeon bowed.

"In our country," the American continued, "there are many opinions as to the secret of your great influence. Would you be good enough to give me your own point of view?"

After a moment's pause, Spurgeon said, "My people pray for me."

His answer showed the humility of the man and the value he placed in the prayers of others. Spurgeon had unfailing faith in prayer. It was always a joy to him to know he was remembered where remembrance is of the most value.

But even the prayers of his people do not provide the full explanation. Many other ministers were happy in the knowledge that their people prayed for them, but they were not Spurgeons.

Dr. Nicoll explained Spurgeon's power in three words: "the Holy Ghost." The Holy Spirit works through humans. Time after time, the Spirit inspires sovereign personalities who become leaders of the masses. This is perhaps the best-known explanation, but even it is incomplete.

Nor is it sufficient to say Spurgeon's greatness stemmed from his personality. Personality may include matters of chance genetics, like fair hair or hazel eyes.

Was it hereditary? Spurgeon was a youthful prodigy. His father, the Reverend John Spurgeon, was frequently away from home, and Charles had the study for his playground. He was said to be "always reading, never digging in the garden or keeping pigeons like other boys, but always books and books." If his mother wanted him, she was sure to find him in the study reading a book.

He soon began to preach. Once when the children were missing, the father found them in the stable, James sitting on the manger, his sisters on straw below, and Charles standing before them in a full flood of oratory.

But there have been many youthful geniuses. Voltaire could read when he was four and composed verses from the cradle. Haller knew the Greek Testament from cover to cover at ten. Humphry Davy was making witty rhymes at five. Descartes was the little philosopher at eight. Bentham was writing Greek and Latin at four and passed his examination at Oxford at ten.

Research in the realm of heredity leaves us with no explanation of Spurgeon's influence.

A great man, it is said, condemns the world to the task of explaining him. There is a fascination in endeavoring to trace the river to its source. Spurgeon was scarcely in his grave before his biographers were arranging his pedigree. (Spurgeon himself said, "I would rather be able to trace my lineage back to the men who suffered for righteousness' sake than to have the blood of the noblest royal family of Europe coursing in my veins.")

Spurgeon was not only a great leader; he lived one of the most public of lives. The things he did, said, and wrote are chronicled. One writer of the period said, "Mr. Spurgeon's biography has been, as it were, constantly written up to date in the current periodic literature of his time. At his death nothing or almost nothing remained to be told respecting him."

This book is not intended simply as a biography but as an attempt to interpret the man and his message. To do this, it is necessary to see the man as he was, not as he appeared in exaggerated affection or in the limelight. It is not my intention to write a eulogy, though that might be pardonable, for like hundreds of ministers, I am indebted to Spurgeon. As a student I sat at his feet in the Pastors' College, and one of the greatest honors of my life was that he called me his friend.

At one time, it was generally expected that Spurgeon would found another Christian denomination. Nearly a thousand ministers had sworn fealty to him, and many thousands in the churches would have responded to his call. Leaders of wealth and influence urged him to become the rallying personality of another communion. But never for a moment did he yield to temptation. He hated separation among Christians.

Was there not something in Spurgeon's wonderful achievements that indicated creative genius? Did he not belong to the category of Athanasius, St. Francis, and others in the little group who, during different periods of world history, have given a new expression of religion and have turned the current of religious history into fresh channels?

An interpretation of the man and his message may contribute to the religious history of England and indeed the world.

TWO

Spurgeon possessed characteristics of the sturdy Hollanders: their love for flowers, their industry, their simple habits. Persecution by the Duke of Alva sent blessings to England, not the least of them the refugees who brought with them new industries. Among these refugees were the Spurgeons who settled in Essex.

The Spurgeon ancestry is a curious mixture: Huguenots, with their passionate love of Protestantism and freedom, and Quakers, with their illumination of the inner light and dislike of all forms and rituals. Job Spurgeon of Dedham in 1677 suffered for the sake of his conscience. A distress warrant was issued against him, his goods were seized, and he was committed to prison for the atrocious crime of attending service out of church. Six years later he was again imprisoned for similar offenses.

C. H. Spurgeon's immediate ancestors were Congregational Independents. His father and grandfather were Congregational ministers. So Huguenots, Quakers, and

Independents all came to flower in the Baptist.

Spurgeon was born at Kelvedon on June 19, 1834. His father was the Reverend John Spurgeon. Charles was the first of seventeen children. His mother was a person of unusual piety and prayerfulness. When John Spurgeon laid one of the cornerstones of the Metropolitan Tabernacle, he related this incident:

I had been from home a great deal, trying to build up weak congregations, and felt that I was somewhat neglecting the religious training of my own children while I toiled for the good of others. I returned home with these feelings. I opened the door and found none of the children about. Going quietly upstairs, I heard my wife's voice; she was engaged in prayer with the children. I heard her pray for them one by one. She came to Charles and specially prayed for him, for he was of high spirit and daring temper. I listened until she had ended, and then I said to myself, "Lord, I will go on with Thy work; the children will be cared for."

Kelvedon and Stambourne were the world of Charles's boyhood. The people there did not have state education, and times were hard. Spurgeon loved the old manse at Stambourne. He wrote:

Oh, the old house at home, who does not love it? The place of our childhood, the old roof-tree, the old cottage. There is no other village in all the world half so good as that particular village. True, the gates, the stiles, and posts have been altered but still there is an attachment to those old houses, the old tree in the park, the old

*ivy-mantled tower. It is not very picturesque, per-
haps, but we love to go to see it. We like to see the
haunts of our boyhood; there is something pleasant in
those old stairs where the clock used to stand, and in
the room where grandmother was wont to bend her
knee and where we had family prayer.*

John Spurgeon moved to Colchester, spending the
week in town keeping books for a coal merchant, and on
Sunday going out to Tollesbury where he ministered to a
little congregation. Charles was at Stambourne with his
grandfather. Charles loved the old Essex town.

According to a writer for the *Christian World*:

*Down in Essex, where I paid a visit last autumn,
near Kelvedon, I heard that Mr. Spurgeon was regarded as a boy as somewhat shy and reticent, if not
indeed somewhat morose. As a matter of fact, no
doubt he was drinking in everything he heard and
saw to be given forth again, however, with good interest when the time came. He was largely brought
up by his grandfather, who was for fifty years Independent minister at Stambourne, a shrewd, clever
old man he appears to have been, whom local tradition regards as the origin, so far as wit and wisdom
are concerned, at all events, of that famous person-
age, John Ploughman.*

Spurgeon grew up in the evangelical faith. He learned
the religious vocabulary of the elderly people who came to
his grandfather's house. He described the religious experience in the terminology of age rather than youth. Many of
his sayings belong to a long-forgotten past.

In the lives of those about him, Spurgeon saw something he did not possess. In his autobiography, he said he had "a clear and sharp sense of the justice of God. Sin, whatever it might be to other people, became to me an intolerable burden. It was not so much that I feared hell as that I feared sin, and all the while I had upon my mind a deep concern for the honor of God's name. I felt that it would not satisfy my conscience if I could be forgiven unjustly, but then there came the question, how could God be just and yet justify me, who had been so guilty? I was worried and wearied with this question, neither could I see any answer to it."

There is something pathetic about the young Spurgeon suffering fear, distress, and grief because of the consciousness of his sins. Understand that Spurgeon was much older than his years, raised among those who commonly talked about the deeper experiences of the soul. God may judge sin by the standard of actual experience. Spurgeon's writing at the time he was seeking the way to Calvary indicates that, like Bunyan's "Pilgrim," Spurgeon had gone through the mire, had touched the bottom of the abyss.

Spurgeon said, "Personally I could never have overcome my own sinfulness. I tried and failed; my evil propensities were too many for me, till in the belief that Christ died for me I cast my guilty soul on Him, and then I received a conquering principle by which I overcame my sinful self."

One of the most beautiful passages in the literature of the soul is Spurgeon's description of an early experience under the conviction of sin:

There was a day, as I took my walks abroad, when I came hard by a spot forever graven upon my memory, for there I saw this Friend, my best, my only Friend, murdered. I stooped down in sad affright and looked at Him. I saw that His hands had been pierced with rough iron nails, and His feet had been rent in the same way. There was misery in His dead countenance so terrible that I scarcely dared to look upon it. His body was emaciated with hunger. His back was red with bloody scourges, and His brow had a circle of wounds about it: Clearly one could see that these had been pierced by thorns. I shuddered, for I had known this Friend full well. He never had a fault; He was the purest of the pure, the holiest of the holy. Who could have injured Him? For He never injured any man: All His life long He "went about doing good." He had healed the sick, He had fed the hungry, He had raised the dead: For which of these works did they kill Him? He had never breathed out anything else but love; and as I looked into the poor sorrowful face, so full of agony, and yet so full of love, I wondered who could have been a wretch so vile as to pierce hands like His.

I said within myself, "Where can these traitors live? Who are these that could have smitten such a One as this?" Had they murdered an oppressor, we might have forgiven them; had they slain one who had indulged in vice or villainy, it might have been his dessert; had it been a murderer and a rebel, or one who had committed sedition, we would have said, "Bury his corpse: Justice has at last given him his due." But when Thou wast slain, my best, my only-beloved, where lodged the traitors? Let me seize them, and they shall be put to death. If there be torments that I can devise, surely they shall endure them all. Oh! what jealousy,

*what revenge I felt! If I might but find these murder-
ers, what would I not do with them! And as I looked
upon that corpse, I heard a footstep and wondered
where it was. I listened, and I clearly perceived that the
murderer was close at hand. It was dark, and I groped
about to find him. I found that, somehow or other,
wherever I put out my hand, I could not meet with
him, for he was nearer to me than my hand would go.
At last I put my hand upon my breast. "I have thee
now," said I; for lo! he was in my own heart; the murderer was hiding within my own bosom, dwelling in
the recesses of my inmost soul. Ah! then I wept indeed,
that I, in the very presence of my murdered Master,
should be harboring the murderer; and I felt myself
most guilty while I bowed over His corpse and sang
that plaintive hymn:*

*'Twas you, my sins, my cruel sins,
His chief tormentors were;
Each of my crimes became a nail,
And unbelief the spear.*

Years later, in September 1855, when Spurgeon was
famous, he preached in a field in King Edward's Road,
Hackney, London. It was a lovely evening. About twelve
thousand people listened to the sermon that lasted nearly an
hour. It later was printed with the title "Heaven and Hell."
Spurgeon said, "I can remember the time when my sins first
stared me in the face. I thought myself the most accursed of
all men. I had not committed any great open transgression
against God, but I recollected that I had been well trained
and tutored, and I thought my sins were thus greater than
the sins of others."

He desperately sought the way of life. He determined to make a pilgrimage to every place of worship in Colchester. He wrote:

I set off, determined to go round to all the chapels, and I went to all the places of worship, and though I dearly venerate the men that occupy those pulpits now and did so then, I am bound to say that I never heard once fully preached the gospel. I mean by that they preached truth, great truth, many good truths that were fitting to many of their congregations, spiritually minded people; but what I wanted to know was: How can I get my sins forgiven? And they never once told me that.

He was raised on books of devotion like Dr. Doddridge's *Life and Progress of Religion in the Soul* and Baxter's *Call to the Unconverted.* Yet he did not know the way.

Finally, what seemed a caprice of the weather brought light and joy to the young seeker. His father recalled, "I was as I remain, in the Congregational Church, and it was to the Independent Church that I drove over every Sunday from Colchester to Tollesbury. Charles was going with me on the Sunday with which I am concerned. However, this particular Sunday turned out to be stormy, and his mother said, 'You had better go to the Primitive Methodist Church,' and he went."

Spurgeon himself recorded:

I sometimes think I might have been in darkness and despair until now had it not been for the goodness of God in sending a snowstorm one Sunday, while I was going to a certain place of worship. When I could go no farther, I turned down a side street and came to a little Primitive Methodist Chapel. In that chapel there may have been a dozen or fifteen people. I had heard of the Primitive Methodists, how they sang so loudly that they made people's heads ache, but that did not matter to me. I wanted to know how I might be saved, and if they could tell me that, I did not care how much they made my head ache.

The minister did not come that morning; he was snowed up, I suppose. At last a very thin-looking man, a shoemaker or tailor or something of that sort, went up into the pulpit to preach.

It is interesting that at least three persons later would claim to be that thin man. Spurgeon regarded the impromptu preacher as a local, not a minister.

The text was: "Look unto Me and be ye saved, all the ends of the earth." The preacher bungled the pronunciation. Spurgeon recorded the opening:

My dear friends, this is a very simple text indeed. It says, "Look." Now lookin' don't take a deal of pains. It ain't liftin' your foot or your finger; it is just "look." Well, a man needn't go to college to learn to look. You may be the biggest fool, and yet you can look. A man needn't be worth a thousand a year to be able to look. Anyone can look; even a child can look. But then the text says, "Look unto Me." Ay! Many on ye are lookin' to yourselves, but it's no use lookin' there. You'll never find any comfort in yourselves. Some look to God the Father. No, look to Him by-and-by. Jesus Christ says, "Look unto Me." Some of ye say, "We must wait for the Spirit's workin'." You have no business with that just now. Look to Christ. The text says, "Look unto Me."

Spurgeon thought the preacher had said all he had to say, when to his great surprise, the thin man looked straight at him and said, "Young man, you look very miserable, and you always will be miserable, miserable in life and miserable in death, if you don't obey my text. But if you obey now, this moment, you will be saved. Young man, look to Jesus Christ. Look. You have nothin' to do but to look and live."

The preaching was crude, but it contained the power of God's salvation. Spurgeon wrote:

I looked until I could almost have looked my eyes away. There and then the cloud was gone, the darkness had rolled away, and that moment I saw the sun, and I could have risen that instant and sung with the most enthusiastic of them, of the precious blood of Christ and the simple faith which looks alone to Him.

There are many ways to the Way. Some find Christ suddenly and dramatically, like Paul on the road to Damascus. Others grow up like Timothy, with the faith of their mothers and grandmothers. John Bunyan's "Pilgrim" toiled with a heavy load until he came to the cross and, in an instant, found release. God's way of bringing the human spirit to Himself cannot be standardized or stereotyped.

Spurgeon's conversion should be a great encouragement to those who preach to small congregations. It was said the authorities at the little chapel were half inclined to cancel the service because of the cold. The worshipers were few. What the world might have missed had that service not taken place!

The boy returned home with the new faith in his heart and a love-light in his eye. He wanted to tell of his wonderful experience, but for hours he was tongue-tied.

"That night," his father said, "we were all at home, and after reading a prayer I said, 'Come, boys, it's time to go to bed.' 'Father,' said Charles, 'I don't want to go to bed yet.' 'Come, come,' said I, whereupon he said he wanted to speak to me. We sat up long into the night, and he talked to me of being saved and told what had taken place that day, and how right glad I was to hear his talk."

Spurgeon wrote of his experience with gratitude and love. He described the work of God's grace on his heart and life with a mellow amazement and joy.

And he believed the experience of conversion must be verified by conduct. He wrote to his mother from Newmarket, where he had gone as an assistant teacher: "I am most happy and comfortable. I read French exercises every night. I have thirty-three houses at present where I leave tracts." To his father, he wrote: "There are but four boarders and about twelve day-boys. I have a nice little mathematical class and have quite as much time for study as I had before. . . . Who can refrain from speaking of the marvelous love of Jesus which I hope has opened mine eyes. Now [that] I see Him I can firmly trust in Him for my eternal salvation."

When Spurgeon came to Christ, he not only saw the vision but, like Isaiah, heard the call to the vocation and answered, "Here am I, send me." He knew how to delight in the Lord. Spurgeon had no sympathy with the easygoing theology that seemed to regard conversion as little more than a change of opinion.

He did not receive instant assurance. He recorded

doubts and fears that were overcome only by prayer and appeals to scripture for truth. He became increasingly sure that all hopes of human salvation rest ultimately on the revealed character of God. It was not human attainment, not what man could achieve, but what God in Christ had done for the world. He feared building his hopes on mortality. He believed the way to clean living was through a changed heart.

If the value of the new birth is to be judged by the life that follows, then Spurgeon's conversion was epoch-making. It contained not only the transforming power of the individual but the seed from which many trees of the Lord grew in all lands.

Spurgeon began at once to share the good news of his conversion with his friends. New ideals developed in his thoughts, new standards of values, and, above all, a passionate longing "to brother all the sons of men." He was both an incomparable advocate and a witness. His childhood was marked with lonely hours and deep dissatisfaction—the divine discontent that will not permit the soul to continue in wrongdoing and disobedience. He wrote:

> *I do from my soul confess that I never was satisfied till I came to Christ; when I was yet a child I had far more wretchedness than ever I have now. I would even add, more weariness, more care, more heartache than I know at this day. I may be singular in this confession, but I make it and know it to be true. Since that dear hour when my soul cast itself on Jesus, I have found solid joy and peace, but before that all those supposed gaieties of early youth, all the imagined joy and ease of boyhood, were but vanity and vexation of spirit to me. That happy day when I found the Savior and learned to cling to His dear*

feet was a day never to be forgotten by me, an obscure child, unknown, unheard of, I listened to the Word of God, and that precious text led me to the cross of Christ. I can testify that the joy of that day was utterly indescribable; I could have leaped, I could have danced. There was no expression, however fanatical, which would have been out of keeping with the joy of my spirit at that hour.

Long afterward, he would return to his favorite subject. He could not understand why preachers did not delight in proclaiming the doctrine of the cross. To him it was meat and drink. He literally delighted in the joy of the Lord. He declared:

I bear witness that never servant had such a Master as I have, never brother had such a kinsman as He has been to me; never spouse had such a husband as Christ has been to my soul; never sinner a better Savior, never soldier a better captain; never mourner a better Comforter than Christ hath been to my spirit. I want none beside Him. In life He is my life, and in death He shall be the death of death; in poverty Christ is my riches, in sickness He makes my bed; in darkness He is my star, and in brightness He is my sun. By faith I understand that the blessed Son of God redeemed my soul with His own heart's blood, and by sweet experience I know that He raised me up from the pit of dark despair and set my feet on the rock. He died for me. This is the root of every satisfaction I have. He put all my transgressions away.

Spurgeon's conversion experience was the foundation of his theory of the death of Jesus. For Spurgeon, there were two sources of authority: the subjective experience of the believer who passes from death to life and enters the family of the twice-born, and the words of the scriptures, wherein Spurgeon found explicit statements concerning the new birth. He could say of his Lord, with all his heart, "He loved me and gave Himself for me."

Spurgeon recognized that the cross, to do its proper work, must be preached. It is not enough to have it represented in art or music; it must be proclaimed. "We preach Christ crucified" was his proud boast. He knew that such preaching had in it the power of God for salvation. The death on the cross is wondrously linked with both moral regeneration and justifying grace.

Spurgeon's experience gave emphasis to his preaching. He believed and therefore declared. Spurgeon always declared the origin of the new birth was in the purpose of God. No human agency was powerful enough to accomplish it. Humans had their parts to play but in response to God's prompting. There could be no salvation except in Christ. Spurgeon stated:

> In the religion of Christ, there are factors even on earth too heavy for one man to carry; there are fruits that have been found so rich that even angel lips have never been sweetened with more luscious wine; there are joys to be had here so fair that even the nectared wine of Paradise can scarcely excel the sweets of satisfaction that are to be found in the earthly banquets of the Lord. I have seen hundreds and thousands who have given their hearts to Jesus, but I never did see one who said he was disappointed with Him. I never

*met one who said Jesus Christ was less than He was
declared to be. When first my eyes beheld Him, when
the burden slipped from off my heavy-laden shoulders,
and I was freed from condemnation, I thought that all
the preachers I had ever heard had not half preached,
they had not told half the beauty of my Lord and
Master, so good, so generous, so gracious, so willing to
forgive; it seemed to me as if they had almost slan-
dered Him, they painted His likeness, doubtless, as
well as they could, but it was a mere smudge compared
with the matchless beauties of His face. All who have
ever seen Him will say the same.*

That early experience in the little chapel at Colchester
decided almost everything for Spurgeon. He was able to
say, "Once I was blind, but now I can see." He proclaimed
the message by which he had been saved, and it was his joy
to see thousands come into the same experience and rejoice
in the same testimony. If his experience is to be judged by
results, then Spurgeon's doctrine of the cross is justified
abundantly.

At Newmarket, young Spurgeon found likable work in
the academy kept by a man named Swindell. He received a
little pay and had the privilege of continuing his own education there, including the study of Greek. During this time
he was influenced greatly by a saintly woman named Mary
King, the cook and general servant in the household. This
big, sturdy soul took an interest in the new tutor and, in the
course of their frequent conversations, found him "well
disposed toward godliness." It is to the great man's credit
that he should receive some of his Calvinism from the
humblest sources. Later, in his first published book *The
Saint and His Savior*, Spurgeon said this woman provided

him with "all the theology I ever needed." She was a strict Baptist. In future hard times, Spurgeon gave her a weekly allowance.

May 3, 1850, his mother's birthday, was the day of Spurgeon's baptism. He said he was led to seek immersion by studying the Church of England Catechism and the Greek New Testament. There was no Baptist church in the Newmarket area, so he went to Isleham Ferry to be baptized in the river Lark with two other disciples. He rose early in the morning, to spend time in prayer before walking the eight miles to the ferry.

He apparently did not join the church at Isleham, perhaps because of the distance from Swindell's school. He simply considered baptism a confession of faith. His parents never shared his Baptist views, but they raised no objection to his baptism. His mother wrote that she often prayed he might become a Christian but not necessarily a Baptist. With characteristic pleasantry, he replied that it was just like the Lord not only to answer prayer but to bestow more than had been asked.

THREE

Ward Beecher said that he who would succeed in life must be careful in the choice of his parents. Had Spurgeon been permitted to choose his parents, he could not have done better than those given to him.

His education began at home. His grandfather, very influential during his early years, taught by example and precept, and his parents followed the same plan.

The training was severe at times. He once wanted a stick of slate pencil for school but had no money to buy it. He related:

> I was afraid of being scolded for losing my pencils so
> often, for I was a careless little fellow and did not
> dare to ask at home. What then was I to do? There
> was a little shop in the place where nuts and tops
> and cakes and balls were sold by old Mrs. Pearson,
> and sometimes I had seen boys and girls get trusted
> by the old lady. I argued with myself that Christmas

was coming and somebody or other would be sure to give me a penny then, and perhaps even a whole silver sixpence. I would therefore get into debt for a stick of slate pencil and be sure to pay at Christmas. I did not feel easy about it but still I screwed up my courage and went into the shop. One farthing was the amount, and as I had never owed anything before my credit was good. The pencil was handed over by a kind dame, and I was in debt. It did not please me much, and I felt as if I had done wrong but I little knew how soon I should smart for it.

Something about his manner must have raised his father's suspicions. His father demanded the truth and then delivered a powerful lecture on the evils of debt, how it might become a habit and bring ruin, disgrace for one's family, and even prison. Poor Charles was only six!

I was marched off to the shop like a deserter marched into barracks, crying bitterly all down the street and feeling dreadfully ashamed, because I thought everybody knew I was in debt. The farthing was paid amid solemn warnings, and the poor debtor was set free like a bird out of a cage.

The lesson sufficed. Spurgeon never got into debt again. The boy knew the value of education. Miss Ann Spurgeon, who lavished affection on her little nephew, declared that at six, when some children could spell words of only one syllable, Charles could read with pointed emphasis. He had many of the privileges denied to most of his classmates. He was under good instructors and did so well that soon he was teaching pupils older than himself.

One of his most prized volumes was a copy of *White's Natural History of Selborne*. It bore this inscription: "Stockwell School, Colchester. Adjudged to Master C. Spurgeon as the first class English prize at the half-yearly examination, December 11, 1844. T. W. Davis, examiner."

One winter morning the tutor at the school arranged the class so that the boys at the bottom sat close to the stove and enjoyed the comforting glow and warmth. Spurgeon was at the top of the class, so the arrangement placed him farthest from the stove. To the schoolmaster's surprise, the boy seemed smitten with dullness; his answers were slow and uncertain. He lost his place and came nearer the warmth. At length he was at the bottom. The teacher was puzzled but he had his suspicions. The order of the class was reversed, with exactly the result the teacher anticipated.

The first night at boarding school, he knelt to pray before going to bed, as was his custom. He was pelted with a shower of slippers and other objects from his fellow boarders. According to one account:

> *Rising from his knees, he strikes out right and left, telling the disturbers of his peace that he must not be interfered with—that he was not accustomed to it, and would not allow it. He then, having knocked several of the boys down, fell upon his knees and finished the prayer without further interruption; nor was he ever again annoyed in like manner.*

Spurgeon himself was largely responsible for the idea among his followers that he lacked educational equipment. John Ploughman was the character he delighted to assume. He belonged to the people. There was about him the healthy smell of the earth and the fragrance of the haystack.

Many of his quaint sayings and odd stories came from the fields and were crude and rustic. But Spurgeon was well-educated. He went to some of the best schools of his day.

His parents sacrificed to give their children the best education they could afford. The school at Colchester, where Charles attended between the ages of eleven and fifteen, was a good classical and commercial establishment, with pupils from the middle class. Henry Lewis, the principal, was a man of high literary attainment. His chief assistant was Leeding, the classical and mathematical tutor.

David Walker, of the college at Maidstone, wrote Spurgeon's father of his observations:

> *Charles is a boy of good ability, good common sense, and very fair acquirements, with steady work he will figure—but his habits are bad—there is a natural carelessness about him which is evident in the very manner in which he puts on his clothes. He wants those little things that would enable a boy of inferior talent to beat him. I have no doubt but he has been beaten by inferior ability and acquirements and will be so again unless he attends to what I am driving into him.*
>
> *His knowledge of Latin, Greek, and mathematics is not so well-founded; he has not had to contend with equals and superiors. He is willing to work and desirous of information. If he used his eyes and ears more and his tongue less, he would sooner gain his object. He improves in this, however, though we have not yet made a smart-looking boy of him. His gait is bad but that improves under an excellent drill and our constant admonition. A man must not only be good and learned, he must look so. Address*

is important in those who have to push their way.

Walker thought better of his pupil as the years passed.

Once at the university level, Spurgeon saw how impossible it was for the poor to obtain knowledge. Elementary schools were few and far between. School attendance was not required. Many people were anxious to keep the working classes in their place; education was regarded as dangerous.

Private evening schools were expensive and generally inefficient, mainly confined to teaching the three R's. In the higher institutions, the best minds in the universities were pressing for drastic reforms. Residence and tuition costs burdened. Oxford admitted that many hopeful students were shut out. A Cambridge degree, with its academic privileges, and the entire Oxford experience were reserved for those who professed membership in the Church of England. Nonconformists like Spurgeon were excluded from studying at Oxford or obtaining degrees at Cambridge.

At the university, the young Puritan found distasteful the social life of Cambridge. He regarded it as a temptation and snare. He loved education but he condemned what he saw of Cambridge:

> *I was for three years a Cambridge man, though I never entered the university. I could not have obtained a degree because I was a Nonconformist; and, moreover, it was a better thing for me to pursue my studies under an admirable scholar and tender friend and to preach at the same time.*

On the advice of friends, Spurgeon decided to start a school of his own. An advertisement that appeared in the local journal indicates his confidence at seventeen:

> *No. 60 Upper Park Street, Cambridge. Mr. C. H.*
> *Spurgeon begs to inform his numerous friends that,*
> *after Christmas, he intends taking six or seven*
> *young gentlemen as day pupils. He will endeavor to*
> *the utmost to impart a good commercial education.*
> *The ordinary routine will include arithmetic, alge-*
> *bra, geometry, and mensuration; grammar and com-*
> *position; ancient and modern history; geography,*
> *natural history, astronomy, scripture, and drawing.*
> *Latin and the elements of Greek and French, if re-*
> *quired. Terms: Five pounds per annum.*

Spurgeon actually became an educational pioneer. He greatly assisted the movement for providing regular and evening classes for working lads. Out of that movement grew the polytechnical colleges with their magnificent curricula and the university extensions.

In 1862, eight years before the House of Commons provided elementary education by the state, Spurgeon established an evening school in the rooms under the Tabernacle. The classes were intended to help young men who wanted to take part in evangelistic work but they were open to all, and no fees were charged. The young men of the tabernacle quickly realized the value of the opportunity, and others, aged sixteen and up, came from all over London. Some of the men were well advanced in years and scarcely could read. These classes enabled manual laborers to obtain free education during their leisure hours.

The curriculum covered elementary subjects and, later, shorthand, bookkeeping, and elementary mathematics. The program succeeded because it combined a bit of recreation with education. The popular lectures were really popular; they were not the scholarly dribble of old men whose words were difficult to hear.

Pitman's shorthand was attracting popular attention. Spurgeon recognized how useful a knowledge of shorthand would be to his students in their ministries. Shorthand classes were begun at the school in 1879 and continued until 1896. They were always free and open to anyone who wanted to enroll.

Occasionally Spurgeon would pay surprise visits to the classes. Once he entered a science class. The tutor paused and welcomed the president and explained the topic of the botanical lecture. To his surprise and the delight of the men, Spurgeon talked intimately on the theme for twenty minutes, then broke off with the remark, "This is not my lecture."

Sometimes he would hold spelling bees, with prizes. The students would put their hats on, and Spurgeon would begin with the first man, posing some simple word which might be spelled in two or three different ways. The students kept their hats on as long as they continued to spell correctly, until at last there would be a solitary hat left. When in a playful mood, Spurgeon would ask for the winner's hat to be passed up to the platform. The prize—usually a book—was placed in the hat.

The struggle for broader evening education continued until London finally had polytechnical and technical institutes that delighted all lovers of education with their range of subjects, efficiency of teaching, and results. Ultimately, any boy or girl with determination could enjoy the pleasures of learning.

In 1899, with the London School Board fully organized and providing better facilities than could be found in private institutions, the trustees of Spurgeon's Pastors' College discontinued evening classes. There is no record of how many students had attended through the years but they clearly numbered in the thousands.

FOUR

Spurgeon began preaching as a child and never lost the habit. "How do you learn to swim?" he once inquired and answered the question himself: "Is it not by swimming?"

He began the ministry as local preacher during his residence at Cambridge. With his friend, Leeding, the accomplished tutor he had known at Colchester, he joined the Church of St. Andrew's Street, made famous by the ministry of the Reverend Robert Hall, the great pulpit orator, and the Reverend Robert Robinson, author of the famous hymn "Come, Thou Fount of Every Blessing."

Of all the stories told of Spurgeon's life at Cambridge, the most interesting are those depicting the romance of local preaching. James Vinter, known as "the Bishop," was the leader of the Local Preachers' Association. He was a shrewd man. He heard of young Spurgeon's success in the Sunday school, where he had been giving the closing address on alternate Sundays. Vinter invited the newcomer Spurgeon to go out to the village of Teversham to accompany the man who was to preach.

Like apostles, the two disciples set out on their journey and talked of the Lord. Spurgeon turned the conversation to the service and prayed his friend would be mightily sustained in his preaching. His companion expressed great surprise, declaring he had never preached in his life and had no intention of doing so today; he simply was accompanying his young brother who was to take the service. If Spurgeon did not feel equal to it, he suggested, they had better turn back.

Spurgeon recalled what "the Bishop" had said to him. It was a cunningly devised sentence. "He just asked me to go over to Teversham, for a young man was to preach there who was not much used to services and very likely would be glad of company."

Spurgeon decided to do his best. As they continued the journey, he prayed for guidance in what he should say. He determined the text: "Unto you therefore which believe He is precious." Years later, he preached at the Music Hall in the Surrey Gardens on the same passage and told the congregation, "This text recalls to my recollection the opening of my ministry. It is about eight years since, as a lad of sixteen, I stood up for the first time in my life to preach the gospel in a cottage to a handful of poor people who had come together for worship."

He chronicled the occasion:

How long or how short it was I cannot now remember. It was not half such a task as I had feared it would be but I was glad to see my way to a fair conclusion and to give out the last hymn. To my own delight I had not broken down nor stopped short in the middle, nor been destitute of ideas, as the desired

*haven was in view. I made a finish and took up the
hymnbook, and to my astonishment a woman's voice
exclaimed, "Bless your dear heart. How old are you?"
I solemnly replied, "You must wait till the service is
over before making any such inquiries. Let us now
sing."*

Little did the listeners imagine the lad standing by the
fireplace in his short jacket with full turndown collar, not
yet sixteen, would become the pulpit orator of the century,
and that the sermon to which they had listened would become historic.

From that time, Spurgeon was much in demand in the
villages around Cambridge. He delighted to find a country cottage or village green to which people might be invited to hear the gospel.

The countryside needed evangelizing almost as much
as any foreign mission field. It is difficult to visualize the
condition of the villages around Cambridge. The Reverend
Desmond Morse-Boycott, a clergyman of the Church of
England, wrote:

*England was a land of closed churches and unstoled
clergy. . . . The parson was often an absentee, not in-
frequently a drunkard. Bishops filled their aprons
with emoluments from sinecures and did but little
work. The rich went to church to doze in upholstered
curtained pews fitted with fireplaces, while the poor
were herded together on uncomfortable benches.*

It is beyond argument that the church was, broadly
speaking, spiritually moribund and discredited utterly. There
were a few earnest men who regretted her imminent collapse.

Despite these deplorable conditions and in spite of all weathers, Spurgeon persevered in his work to tell the story that transforms the world to the people of the countryside.

I must have been a singular-looking youth on wet evenings. During the last year of my stay in Cambridge, when I had given up my office as usher, I was wont to sally forth every night in the week except Saturday, and to walk three, five, or perhaps eight miles out and back on my preaching excursions, and when it rained I dressed myself in waterproof leggings and mackintosh coat and a hat with a waterproof covering, and carried a dark lantern to show me the way across the fields. I had many adventures.

Spurgeon loved nature in all its moods. He enjoyed tramping the road in the middle of a storm.

When God is abroad I love to walk out in some wide space and to look up and mark the opening gates of heaven, as the lightning reveals far beyond and enables me to gaze into the unseen. I like to hear my Father's voice vibrate in the thunder.

He would go to a cottage and amaze the occupants by asking permission to hold a service in their room. If that were denied and the weather permitted, he would go around to the houses, inviting the people to come out into the open and join in the worship of God. He found peculiar pleasure in talking to the rustic crowds who formed the circle to listen with open-eyed amazement to the boy preacher.

On one occasion he tramped through the rain and found a congregation waiting. It was haying time, and he took for his text: "He shall come down like the rain upon the mown grass, as showers that water the earth."

> *Surely we had the blessing as well as the inconvenience. I was sufficiently wet and my congregation must have been drenched but they stood it out, and I never heard that anybody was the worse in health, though I thank God I have heard of souls brought to Jesus under that discourse.*

Spurgeon never lost his love for local preaching. And he knew enough of the history of the church to convince him of the value of the layman's testimony. The early church was a church of witnesses. Witnessing to the saving power of Christ is not a task committed to a minister alone; it is an obligation resting on each disciple. The teacher in the school is charged with finding an opportunity to tell the story. The soldier must confess his allegiance within the regiment. The rich in their mansions and the poor in their cottages, if they have found the Lord, are under the same obligation to share the blessing with others.

All the time the young preacher was learning by doing, he regarded himself as a lay preacher. He does not seem to have considered that he was being prepared for the ministry. He insisted on the privilege and duty of laymen testifying to their Lord's saving and keeping power.

"Bishop" Vinter of the Lay Preachers' Society had jurisdiction over thirteen villages. In these villages, Spurgeon was to be found night after night. He loved the work.

It was his custom to rise early in the morning for a quiet time of prayer and meditation. He would decide on a text or subject and meditate on it when he was free from teaching. He stated:

> What I had gathered by my studies during the day I handed out to a company of villagers in the evening and was myself greatly profited by the exercise. I always found it good to say my lesson when I had learned it. Children do so; it is equally good for preachers, especially if they say their lesson by heart. In my young days I fear I said many odd things and made many blunders but my audiences were not hypercritical, and no newspaper writers dogged my heels; so I had a happy training ground in which by continual practice I attained such degree of ready speech as I now possess.
>
> There is no way of learning to preach which can be compared with preaching itself. If you want to swim, you must get into the water, and if you at first make a sorry exhibition, never mind; for it is by swimming as you can that you learn to swim as you should. We ought to be lenient with beginners, for they will do better by and by. If young speakers in Cambridge had been discouraged and silenced, I might not have found my way here, and therefore I shall be the last to bring forth a wet blanket for any who sincerely speak for Christ, however humble may be their endeavors. The fear of there being too many preachers is the last that will occur to me.

When he settled in London later, Spurgeon began the Lay Preachers' Association which met each week for training. Often the tabernacle lecture hall was crowded with eager young men.

Many Cambridge villagers who listened to the boy preacher not only were impressed; their lives were changed. Hyper-Calvinists and others sometimes protested that the lad was either too broad or too narrow but many rejoiced in the message that was, to them, the word of life.

In *Lectures to My Students*, Spurgeon devoted considerable attention to open-air preaching:

> I am sure that if we could persuade our friends in the country to come out a good many times in the year and hold a service in a meadow or in a shady grove or on the hillside or on a common, it would be all the better for the usual hearers. The mere novelty of the place would freshen their interest and wake them up. The slight change of scene would have a wonderful effect upon the more somnolent. See how mechanically they go out again. They fall into their seats as if at last they have found a resting place. They rise to sing with an amazing effort; they drop down before you have time for a doxology at the close of the hymn because they did not notice it was coming. What logs some regular hearers are; many of them are asleep with their eyes open, after sitting a certain number of years in the same old spot where the pews, pulpit, and gallery and all things else, are always the same, except that they get a little dirtier and dingier every week, where everybody occupies the same position forever and ever, and the minister's face, voice, tone, are much the same from January to December. You get to feel the holy quiet of the scene and listen to what is going on as though it were addressed to the dull, cold ear of death.

With that description, he contrasted the scene in the open air. He loved to preach in nearby Minster Lovell in Oxfordshire, afterward called Spurgeon's Tabernacle. It was an ideal preaching place.

The inner temple consisted of a large square out of which the underwood and smaller trees had been cut away, while a sufficient number of young oaks had been left to rise to a considerable height and then overshadow us with their branches. Here was a truly magnificent cathedral, a temple not made with hands, of which we might truly say:

*"Father, Thy hand
Hath reared these venerable columns, Thou
Didst weave this verdant roof."*

I have never, either at home or on the Continent, seen architecture which could rival my cathedral. "Lo, we heard of it at Ephratah: we found it in the fields of the wood." The blue sky was visible through our clerestory, and from the great window at the further end the sun smiled upon us toward evening.

The young preacher's fame found its way into the chapels, where he was invited to preach on special occasions. The little church at Waterbeach, a thriving community, was five miles away. Prosperity enabled the people to indulge their tastes in undesirable ways. When Spurgeon occupied its pulpit, there were some who objected to boys being elevated to the pastorate. But the invitation was given and accepted, and Spurgeon, like the Vicar of Wakefield, became "passing rich on forty pounds a year."

Deacon Coe said of the boy preacher's first service at Waterbeach, "He talked amazingly, like a man a hundred years old in Christian experience." Many came to hear the youth out of curiosity—and remained to give God thanks.

Spurgeon's intense evangelism did more than raise opposition; it brought about something like a revolution in the village. Bad times came, economically. Spurgeon described the village:

> *Did you ever see poor wretched beings that once were men standing or rather leaning against the posts of alehouses or staggering along the street? Have you ever looked into the houses of the people and beheld them as dens of iniquity at which your soul stood aghast? Have you ever seen the poverty and degradation of the inhabitants and sighed over it? . . . I knew just such a village, perhaps in some respects one of the worst in England, where many an illicit still was yielding its noxious liquor to a manufacturer without payment of the duty to the government, and where in connection with that evil all manner of riot and iniquity was rife.*

Not a promising outlook for the boy pastor—but his work soon began to tell. The little thatched chapel was crammed, and some of the worst in the village, who had been the curse of the parish, became its blessing. Noted Spurgeon:

> *It was a pleasant thing to walk through that place when drunkenness had almost ceased, when debauchery in the case of many was dead, when men and women went forth to labor with joyful hearts, singing the praises of the everliving God, and when*

*at sunset the humble cottager called his children to-
gether, read them some portion from the book of
truth, and then together they bent their knees in
prayer to God.*

The first of the many converts was a poor woman.
When the pastor heard her story, he said, "I felt like the boy
who had earned his first guinea, or like a diver who had been
down to the depths of the sea and brought up a rare pearl."

The ministry at Waterbeach was good preparation for
what would follow. It allowed time for study, which Spurgeon used well. He spent his mornings meditating and
writing, preparing for the pulpit. It would have been easy
for the young preacher to settle down in indolence, using
the outlines of past sermons. But he was a worker, not content with less than the best he could do.

His father, anxious for him to receive the best possible
education, urged him to apply to Stepney College (later
known as Regent's Park College). Charles declined, explaining in an 1852 letter to his father:

*I want to tell you why I think it wise not to go to
college now. I have waited because (1) I wanted to
get a little more to tell you. (2) I do not want to appear to desire to go to college at your expense. I do
not want to go until I can pay for it [on] my own, or
until friends offer to help, because I do not want to
burden you.*

*It is said by almost all friends that I ought to go
to college. I have no very great desire for it, in fact
none at all. Yet I have made it a matter of prayer
and I trust, yea, I am confident, God will guide me.
Of course you are my only director and guide in these*

matters. Your judgment always has been best; you must know best. But perhaps you will allow me just to state my own opinion, not because I shall trust in it but only that you may see my inclination. I think then (with all deference to you) that I had better not go to college yet, at least not just now, for

1. Whatever advantages are to be derived from such a course of study I shall be more able to improve when my powers are more developed than I can at present. When I know more I shall be more able to learn.

2. Providence has thrown me into a great sphere of usefulness, a congregation of often 450, a loving and praying church and an awakened audience. Many we hope already own that the preaching has been with power from heaven. Now ought I to leave them?

3. In a few years' time I hope to improve my purse, so as to be at no expense to you, or at least not for all. I should not like to know that you were burdening yourself for me. I should love to work my own way as much as possible. I know you like this feeling.

4. I am not uneducated. I have many opportunities of improvement now; all I want is more time but even that Mr. Leeding would give me, if it were so arranged. I have plenty of practice and do we not learn to preach by preaching? You know what my style is. I fancy it is not very collegelike. Let it be never so bad; God has blessed it, and I believe He yet will. All I do right He does in me, and the might is of Him. I am now well-off. I think as well-off as anyone of my age and I am sure quite as happy. If I

*were in need I think the people may be able to raise
more for me. Now shall I throw myself out and trust
to Providence as to whether I shall ever get another
place, as soon as I leave college.*

*5. But no. I have said enough, you are to judge,
not I. I leave it to God and yourself but still I should
like you to decide in this way. Of course I have a
will, and you know it but I say not mine but your
will and God's will. I have just acknowledged the
letter and said that I could make no reply until I had
consulted my friends.*

*I hope you will excuse my scrawl, for, believe
me, I am fully employed. Last night I thought of
writing but was called out to see a dying man, and I
thought I dare not refuse. The people at W. would
not like to get even a hint of my leaving them. I do
not know why they love me, but they do. It is the
Lord's doing. . . .*

The work went merrily at Waterbeach. The income
was forty-five pounds a year, though twelve shillings a
week had to be paid for rent for two rooms. Some members of the congregation, knowing his difficulties, helped
the young pastor either with money or food. He was determined to continue his work there. Like Augustine and
Paul, he had heard a voice bidding him not to seek greater
things for himself.

He noted:

*I can testify that great numbers of humble country-
folk accepted the Savior's invitation, and it was delightful to see what a firm grip they afterwards had
of the verities of the faith. Many of them became*

*perfect masters in divinity. I used to think sometimes
that if they had degrees who deserved them, diplo-
mas would often be transferred and given to those
who hold the plough handle or work at the carpen-
ter's bench, for there is often more divinity in the little finger of a ploughman than there is in the whole
body of our modern divines. Don't they understand
divinity? someone asks. Yes, in the letter of it but as
to the spirit and the life of it, D.D. often means dou-
bly destitute.*

There were candid critics at Waterbeach. In the early
days, Potto Brown, the miller at Houghton, invited Spurgeon to preach in his chapel and be his weekend guest.
When they sat down to breakfast, the host said, "We always
provide two eggs for the minister's breakfast on Sunday
morning. The phosphorus in them feeds the brain, and it
looks as though you will need plenty of mental nourish-
ment today."

After awhile, Brown put the question: "Young man,
whoever persuaded you that you could preach?"

After lengthy explanation, Brown asked whether Spurgeon had gone to live at Waterbeach.

"No, sir, I am at Cambridge, where I teach in a school."

"Oh, then," Brown said, "you're only an apprentice boy
at present, just trying your hand at preaching. Your ministry
is a sort of off-hand farm to be cultivated at odd times."

Another time, Spurgeon was invited to preach at
Cottenham. The old minister received him with surprise.
"I shouldn't have asked you here had I known you were
such a bit of a boy, yet the people have been pouring into
the place all the morning in wagons and dickey-carts and
all kinds of vehicles. More fools they." The old man was

concerned the boy would not be able to "last out" to the usual sermon length.

At Isleham, where he was baptized, Spurgeon was asked to take the morning and evening services; another preacher would have the afternoon. Only seven people attended in the morning. But Spurgeon did his best for them—and the church was overcrowded at the evening service.

His brother James occasionally went with him on his preaching excursions, sometimes driving him in a pony-drawn chaise to the place of worship. James recorded that Charles was not only popular but was a preacher of many dimensions.

The rustic congregations knew the ring of sincerity. They might gape at displays of rhetorical fireworks but they were not moved by them. As they listened to the seventeen-year-old, they were amazed at the depth of his experience. Many things he said pointed to his industrious reading of the Puritan fathers—but Spurgeon made the experience his own. He did not simply read experimental theology with unflagging interest and profit; he was so sensitized in spirit that he took on the experiences of others and lived them until they became his own.

"Who is this Spurgeon?" was being asked in the villages and towns. Spurgeon knew the value of publicity. He did not contradict the quaint things that were reported about him, and his fame spread. Yet he was reminded, as by a voice from heaven: "Seekest thou great things for thyself? Seek them not."

He was not blind to the advantages of college training. He was ever urging students to obtain all the education possible. But for himself, he felt he must make up by personal effort what he would miss from tutelage. This decision was the turning point of his career. It compelled him to examine his motives: What was he seeking? He was not content until he could expose the innermost desires of his heart in the presence of the Lord.

He remained at Waterbeach, with his little rustic crowd, sure his pathway had been made clear. He had found the light to his feet, the guide to his path. He never wavered in his determination to forego college and acquire whatever knowledge came his way. He worked with a will, reading carefully the writings of the pulpit masters. Rising early in the morning, he spent hours in quiet study and, in the evening, tested his knowledge before a congregation.

It was impossible for a preacher of Spurgeon's quality to remain unknown. Some of his flock at Waterbeach predicted he soon would be in a prominent pulpit—but it never occurred to them it would be in one of the oldest churches in the empire's capital city.

The invitation to a London church came about through an attack on the young preacher at a meeting of the Cambridge Sunday School Union in 1853. Two other ministers, much older than Spurgeon, were to speak. Spurgeon was called to give the first address. He described:

> *I do not now recollect anything that I said on that occasion but I have no doubt that I spoke in my usual straightforward fashion. I do not think there was anything in my remarks to cause the other speakers to turn upon me so savagely as they did when it came to their turn to address the large gathering. One of them in particular was very personal, and also most insulting in his observations, specially referring to my youth, and then in what he seemed to regard as a climax, saying it was a pity that boys did not adopt the scriptural practice*

> *of tarrying at Jericho till their beards were grown*
> *before they tried to instruct their seniors.*
>
> *Having obtained the chairman's permission, I*
> *reminded the audience that those who were bidden*
> *to tarry at Jericho were not boys but full-grown men*
> *whose beards had been shaved off by their enemies as*
> *the greatest indignity they could be made to suffer*
> *and who were, therefore, ashamed to return home*
> *until their beards had grown again. I added, "The*
> *true parallel to their case could be found in a minis-*
> *ter who, through falling into open sin, had disgraced*
> *his sacred calling, and so needed to go into seclusion*
> *for a while until his character had to some extent*
> *been restored."*

Spurgeon's remark struck home. He learned afterward that the critical minister was not true to his calling.

Among those present was George Gould of Loughton. He was greatly impressed by Spurgeon's address and his unusual courage. Gould knew one of the deacons of New Park Street Chapel in London, Thomas Olney, and urged that Spurgeon be invited for a Sunday. For a while, Olney apparently forgot all about it. Reminded, he consulted with the church officers. A letter was sent to Spurgeon at Waterbeach.

On the last Sunday morning of November 1853 the boy, wearing the turndown collar and short jacket, found his way through the mist to his little church as usual. The walk excited him, and he was eager to get on with the service. He turned to select the hymns. On the hymnal was a letter bearing a London postmark. Curious, he opened it. It contained a formal invitation to occupy the pulpit at New Park Street, where Dr. Rippon once had been minister.

Spurgeon thought it was a mistake and passed the letter to one of his friends. The old man looked at it and shook his head. He was not surprised but sad. "Had it been Cottenham or St. Ives or Huntingdon," he said, "I should not have wondered at all. But going to London is rather a great step from this little place."

Spurgeon replied to London, regretting his inability to accept the invitation but offering to serve on December 11. He wrote:

> *I have been wondering very much how you could have heard of me, and I think I ought to give some account of myself, lest I should come and be out of my right place. Although I have been more than two years minister of a church which has in that time doubled, yet my last birthday was only my nineteenth. I have hardly ever known what the fear of man means, and have all but uniformly had large congregations, and frequently crowded ones but if you think my years would unqualify me for your pulpit, then by all means do not let me come. The great God, my helper, will not leave me to my rest.*

The letter was sent with much fear and trembling. The answer came, accepting his December 11 appearance. Spurgeon's humility is seen in the correspondence. He never appeared to lack confidence in God or himself but he was a lowly minded man—sure of himself simply because he had no doubts concerning his God. He believed that whatever God called him to undertake, God would give him strength to carry through.

There were many sad hearts in the village chapel when it became known the pastor had been invited to preach in a London church. The wise old saints shook their heads and declared they always had felt the boy would go to London but he was going too soon.

But others were certain London was Spurgeon's destiny.

FIVE

Sunday, December 11, 1853, is one of the most memorable dates in the history of modern Baptists. It is one of the great dates in the history of Christianity in England. C. H. Spurgeon preached at New Park Street Chapel for the first time. The newspapers took no note of the day, except that it was cold and dull, without rain.

Even the religious papers seemed hardly aware of Spurgeon's existence. It took a year for the Baptist journal, the *Freeman*, to discover the preacher. During that time he had become the sensation of the metropolis.

The Baptist Union Annual Assembly in 1854 made no reference to Spurgeon. It seemed preoccupied with decreasing growth rate. The denomination was fragmented and offered little inspiration to the new minister.

Spurgeon arrived in the city on a Saturday afternoon. It was a sullen day with a touch of east wind that seemed to pierce every garment. He made his way through dirty streets and narrow alleys to Queen's Square, Bloomsbury, where the deacons had arranged for him to stay at a little boardinghouse.

He never forgot the impressions of that Saturday. He went to the boardinghouse and found "young gentlemen" who, after the meal, sat around the fire in the dingy room that was dining room at midday, drawing room in the afternoon, and lounge in the evening. The furniture was uncomfortable and well-worn. The young gentlemen evidently intended to take the courage out of the newcomer. They seemed greatly tickled that the boy should presume to be a preacher, and that he actually intended to preach in one of the city's historic pulpits.

The temperature in the room became unbearable, and Spurgeon excused himself and went to bed. He was shown into a little cupboard room over the front door and lay down—but not to sleep.

> *On the narrow bed I tossed in a solitary misery and found no pity. Pitiless was the grind of the cabs in the street, pitiless the recollection of the young city clerks whose grim propriety had gazed upon my rusticity with such amusement; pitiless the spare room which scarcely afforded me space to kneel; pitiless even the gas lamps which seemed to wink at me as they flickered amid the. . .darkness. I had no friends in all that city full of human beings but felt myself to be among strangers and foreigners and hoped to be helped through the scrape into which I had been brought and to escape safely to the serene abodes of Cambridge and Waterbeach, which then seemed to be Eden itself.*

At breakfast the young men renewed the conversation. Where was he to preach? Oh, New Park Street—the other side of the water, in Southwark. How would he get there? Walk? Well, it was a considerable distance. He should go along Holborn Hill to Blackfriars, and then through the lanes at the foot of Southwark Bridge. Was he going as he was, in those baggy trousers? He denied that his trousers were baggy; they were only full at the knees.

He started out. Why had he come to London? Was he after all seeking great things for himself?

It is not surprising that Spurgeon was a Calvinist. Almost all our great people have confessed to a consciousness that they were being compelled along the way they seemed to choose for themselves. Perhaps it is true that in the great moments of destiny, there is no question of choice; there is the Divine urge.

Spurgeon trudged the streets to his Thermopylë, wondering, praying, fearing, hoping, believing. "I felt all alone, and yet not alone; expectant of Divine help and inwardly borne down by my sense of the need of it." He was a lonely pilgrim on the way to his Calvary, torn between the desire to be back in the village pulpit and the passion for adventure. One text returned to his mind many times during that walk: "He must needs go through Samaria."

Already Spurgeon did not like London, though he had seen only the merest indication of the hardness of city life in which he would make his home. The city was described by Sidney Webb in *London Education*:

> *Nothing. . .can give an adequate vision of the abominations that, within the memories of men still living, prevailed in all the working-class quarters— two-thirds of the whole child population growing up not only practically without schooling or religious influences of any kind but also indescribably brutal and*

immoral; living amid the unthinkable filth of vilely
overcrowded courts unprovided either with water
supply or sanitary conveniences, existing always at
the lowest level of physical health, and constantly
decimated by disease; incessantly under temptation
by the flaring gin palaces which alone relieved the
monotony of the mean streets and dark alleys to
which they were doomed; graduating almost in-
evitably into vice and crime amid the now incredible
street life of an unpoliced metropolis.

Spurgeon had read something of the history of New
Park Street Chapel but he was not prepared for the grim
building upon which he gazed timidly. He said:

It seemed to my eyes to be a large, ornate, and im-
posing structure, suggesting an audience wealthy and
critical, and far removed from the humble folk to
whom my ministry had been sweetness and light. It
was early, so there were no persons entering, and
when the set time was fully come, there were no
signs to support the suggestion raised by the exterior
of the building, and I felt that by God's help I was
not out of my depth and was not likely to be in so
small an audience.

Inside the building were traces of a great past. There
was Dr. Gill's chair, upon which Spurgeon sat in awe. There
were portraits. Later he would remember details but on that
fateful morning he only could feel how marvelous it was to
be in that vestry, sitting in the chair of the learned man
whose shoes he would have counted it an honor to clean.

Dr. Gill's ministry extended from 1720 to 1771; Dr.

Rippon followed him until 1836, so between them their pastorates covered 116 years.

Dr. Gill was one of the most learned men of his day, easily the most learned of his denomination. He came from Kettering, where he was born in 1697. At London, he undertook an *Exposition of the Whole New Testament* in three volumes. When Marischal College in Aberdeen conferred upon him the Doctor of Divinity, he said, "I never thought it nor bought it nor sought it." Gill was controversial, contending with Wesley and others.

Dr. Rippon, whose hymnbook became a standard, was different. He devoted much attention to the music of the church and compiled a supplement to Watts's hymns. He also edited the *Baptist Annual Register* and took a prominent part in denominational concerns.

The time came for the service to begin. Spurgeon faced not a multitude but a mere handful of people dotted about the church—a much smaller congregation than the one at Waterbeach. It seemed New Park Street was living in its past.

Spurgeon preached from the words, "Every good gift and every perfect gift is from above and cometh down from the Father of lights, with whom is no variableness neither shadow of turning." His treatment of the subject was fresh but hardly novel. He described the majestic figure of the Father of lights:

> *Yon sun has shone on my cradle, it will beam on my deathbed, and cast a gleam into my grave. So doth God, the beneficent, gild our path with sunshine. Earth were a gloomy vault without Him; with Him, it is light and joyous, the porch of a still more blissful state.*

At the close of the service, the congregation was puzzled. This young man was unlike any supply pastor. His voice had a haunting charm, clear and unusually powerful. Despite his youthfulness, he was wonderfully mature, and his knowledge of the Bible was very welcome.

At the evening service, the morning congregation returned and brought others with them. There had been considerable talk about the newcomer. Was he eccentric or natural?

The evening subject was from Revelation: "They are without fault before the throne of God." Spurgeon had used the theme before; in fact, the sermon in almost every way had been preached to his country crowd.

The people were thrilled. They wanted to know when he was coming again. Why not invite him for a month?

The theme was the secret of the sermon. What might have happened if, instead of preaching Christ crucified, Spurgeon had chosen one of the hundred questions being discussed at the hour? Like Paul, Spurgeon had determined to know nothing except Jesus Christ crucified. Whatever text he might begin with, it led to the cross. On that first Sunday in New Park Street, he had "let himself go" with his all-absorbing theme. Regardless of whether he was invited back, the people would know he gave first place to the gospel.

The preacher was a little hard on those who in their own opinion were faultless but who easily discovered many faults in their neighbors. It is interesting to note that among the faults Spurgeon emphasized were those of the Pharisees, the sham sinners "who talk very daintily of being sinners. I have no good opinion of them. John Berridge said that he kept a rod for sham beggars, and I will keep one for these pretenders."

He rebuked those in the churches who sang sweetly but lived poorly. He approved those who sought unity.

That night settled the question of Spurgeon's future, as well as the history of the church to which he preached. One of the deacons had brought with him a young lady who was greatly taken with the preacher—who afterward took her for better or for worse.

Some parishioners wanted a church meeting immediately to issue an invitation. Others urged that he serve as a supply pastor for a Sunday or two. Deacon Olney tentatively suggested an early decision.

"No," Spurgeon said, "I can't afford it."

"Why not?" asked Olney's son William—father of a latter-day evangelist.

"I have two students who might leave me if they were left too long."

"How much do they pay you?"

"Ten pounds."

Taking two five-pound notes from his pocket, William Olney said, "There's the money. We want you here."

Thus C. H. Spurgeon found his Jonathan, and William Olney his David.

When Spurgeon returned to the boardinghouse, he walked erect. There was no fear in his eye as he faced the young gentlemen who wanted to tell him about the preachers they had heard.

He did not return alone. He was accompanied by Joseph Passmore, who afterward became the publisher of Spurgeon's works.

The little bed in the box room over the door did not seem so small, and the noises outside were strangely hushed. Somehow, he was assured all was well. He was not an adventurer seeking great things for himself; he was willing to be where his Master wanted him.

He wrote to his father:

> *Should I be settled at London I will come and see you often. I do not anticipate going there with much pleasure. I am contented where I am but if God has more for me to do, then let me go and trust in Him.*
>
> *The London people are rather higher in Calvinism than myself but I have succeeded in bringing one church to my own views and will trust with Divine assistance to do the same with another. I am a Calvinist, I love what someone called "glorious Calvinism," but Hyperism is too hot-spiced for my palate.*

He seemed doubtful about the theology of the people at New Park Street: "It is Calvinism they want in London, and any Arminian preaching will not be endured." But he was taken by the chapel itself: "It is one of the finest in the denomination, somewhat in the style of our Cambridge museum."

And London surely intrigued him. He spent Monday touring the city. It must have thrilled him to stand in the yard of the House of Commons, from where the eloquently spoken word had determined the destinies of nations. Across the road was the Abbey, with its wealth of history in marble. At Trafalgar Square, groups of the ill clad and ill fed stared at the fountains that did not play. He crossed to the park, with its windswept trees and roads thick with autumn leaves.

In the afternoon he went to St. Paul's, climbed to the top, and, like all visitors from the country, was amazed to hear his own voice in the Whispering Gallery. On the famous booksellers' row he bought *Scott's Commentary*, then went down the Strand.

There was the Cock Tavern, where some of the best and greatest in English literature used to meet. The little house still provided good coffee, as in the days of Dr. Johnson and his friends.

Spurgeon had the gift of journalism, and Fleet Street—the tongue, if not the brain, of the world—must have inspired him. Little did the country lad dream that in a few months Fleet Street would send reporters to his services, eager to report what he said and did!

At the street market were barrows of books and little stalls. Almost anything could be bought, from a box of pins to trousers to meat and fish, bread and confectionery.

What a day for a young man from the country! From his sightseeing he gathered a storehouse of incidents and illustrations for years to come.

Returning to Cambridge, he was affected by the sorrow among his people at Waterbeach. They realized their happy association with their lay pastor was nearing an end. His hour of destiny had struck, and he must move.

The young pastor was not eager to go. He was held by the harmony at Waterbeach and the devotion of the people. But when he returned to preach at New Park Street again, there was a quiet assurance that gave him inward peace.

He accepted an invitation to preach two Sundays in January. The church decided to invite him for six months. Only five people voted against the invitation; the overwhelming majority were enthusiastic.

Spurgeon did not like the idea of a six-month commitment. He wrote:

After well weighing the matter I dare not accept an unqualified invitation for so long a time. My objection is not to the length of the time of probation but it ill becomes a youth to promise to preach to a London congregation so long until he knows them and they know him. I would engage to supply for three months of that time and then, should the congregation fail or the church disagree, I would reserve myself to liberty, without breach of engagement, to retire, and you could, on your part, have the right to dismiss me without seeming to treat me ill. Should I see no reason for so doing and the church still retain their wish for me, I can remain the other three months, either with or without the formality of a further invitation; but even during that time (the second three months), I should not like to regard myself as a fixture, in case of ill success but would only be a supply, liable to a fort-night's dismissal or resignation.

Perhaps this is not businesslike, I do not know: But this is the course I should prefer if it would be agreeable to the church. Enthusiasm and popularity are often the crackling of thorns and soon expire. I do not wish to be a hindrance if I cannot be a help.

New Park Street wanted the preacher at once but he would not agree. Finally they accepted his suggestion that, since he had given them four Sundays, he should give Waterbeach four. He did not discuss the question of stipend, simply saying, "Pecuniary matters I am well satisfied with."

The little church at Waterbeach had some hopes that in three months the pastor would be tired of London and more than a little homesick. Some of the people dared to express the desire that London would be tired of Spurgeon, and he would come back wiser, if a little saddened, by the experience.

But Spurgeon's success in London began before he or the church officers realized what was happening. The church filled rapidly. Prayer meetings were revived, and there were constant applications for membership from those who had been brought to the Lord under the new ministry.

The church voted to extend a permanent invitation immediately. Their resolution stated that during Spurgeon's brief ministry, "we regard the extraordinary increase in the attendance upon the means of grace, both on Lord's Day and week evenings, combined with the manifest fact that his ministry has secured the general approbation of the members, as an encouraging token that our Heavenly Father has directed His way toward us in answer to the many prayers we have offered up for a suitable pastor— and as there are several inquirers desirous of joining our fellowship, we consider it prudent to secure as early as possible his permanent settlement among us."

Nine days later, Spurgeon accepted by letter, noting:

I ask your cooperation in every good work, in visiting the sick, in bringing in inquirers, in mutual edification. Oh that I may be no injury to you but a lasting benefit. I have no more to say saving this: that if I have expressed myself in these few words in a manner unbecoming my youth and inexperience, you will not impute it to arrogance but forgive my mistake.

Spurgeon was settled in a London pastorate, in a big, gloomy old church that had been the home of great traditions and large cobwebs. It sometimes had been discussed whether the building, in such an out-of-the-way location with a great brewery on one side and a vinegar distillery on the other, should be sold.

But the scene was soon to change. Spurgeon and his deacons might have been appalled if they could have seen the future. Few London churches (six of them Baptist) had more than three hundred members, and congregations had dwindled for years. The faithful deplored the decline of interest in religion and the increasing disregard for the Lord's Day. It was not a time when ministers swayed public opinion. The outlook was gloomy.

It was the darkness before dawn.

SIX

Unchurched London soon responded to the preacher from the Fens. He was a living voice, not an echo of the dead past. Unlike the popular preachers of the day, he did not simply attract members of other churches but made his appeal to men and women of all types, from highest to lowest. He was the theme of conversation and criticism.

From the first, Spurgeon obviously did not fit into any of the categories of ministers in the metropolis. By the staid and orthodox, he was regarded as an innovator and opposed at every new departure. In one regard, these critics were right: There was nothing conventional about Spurgeon's personality or method. He talked the language of the common people, colloquial but not vulgar. Heart thoughts, he declared, are the best thoughts and should be spoken so people can understand them.

A critic wrote:

*To the pith of Jay and plainness of Rowland Hill he
adds much of the familiarity, not to say the coarseness,
of the Huntingtonian or the ultra-Calvinists. "It has
been my privilege," Spurgeon says, "to give more
prominence in the religious world to those old doctrines of the gospel." But the traits referred to present
themselves in shapes and with accompaniments which
forbid the notion of imitation, and favor the opinion
of a peculiar bent. Neither in the style and structure
nor in handling is there appearance of art, study, or
elaboration. "This," he says, "I am sure of: I tell you all
I know and speak right on. I am no orator but tell you
what springs up from my heart."*

But Spurgeon was an orator. One of the most famous
dramatic critics of the day, Sheridan Knowles, described
him as "absolutely perfect in his oratory." Knowles declared
that had he been on the stage, Spurgeon easily would have
filled the largest theater.

Spurgeon was dramatic to his fingertips. He not only
uttered the words; he acted them. He made the simple things
come alive. Every moment contributed. When he preached,
the whole man was engaged in conveying the message. A
bitter critic, probably James Wells, wrote in the *Earthen
Vessel* in January 1855:

*The laws of oratory have been well studied, and he
suits the action to his words. This mode of public
speaking was, in the theaters of ancient Greece, carried
to such an extent that one person had to speak the
words and another had to perform the gestures and
suit with every variety of face and form the movement
of the subject in hand. Mr. Spurgeon has caught the*

idea, only with this difference, that he performs both parts himself.

In later years, before a service he might seem somber, the eyes dull, the lips tightly pressed. But when he rose to speak and warmed to his subject, the eyes lit up until they flashed flame. The whole countenance was transformed.

Spurgeon rather liked the idea that he was breaking the cobwebs of convention. He shocked the people of Scotland by declaring they did not understand him. "Why, bless your hearts," he said, "I would preach standing on my head, if I thought I could convert your souls, rather than preach on my feet. I am not very particular about how I preach." Later, when accused of being a "ranting fellow," he said, "My motto is *Cedo nulli*—'I yield to none.'" He flatly refused to be "cribbed, cabined, and confined" by the rules of the time.

The first great breach of ministerial etiquette arose over the question of ordination. He had accepted the pastorate of New Park Street Chapel with all its traditions and decorum but he had not been properly ordained. An ordination service was suggested to him, perhaps with a tea and public meeting. The prayer could be offered by a London minister and the charge to the church and to Spurgeon given by two others.

Spurgeon replied to the idea in a long letter to the church secretary. He objected to an ordination service on various grounds, holding that his ministry had been recognized by God and he needed no further authorization. He did not accept the doctrine of delegating power from minister to minister. He believed every church had a right to choose its own minister, and he certainly needed no assistance from others in appointing him to the office. If the church insisted, he would submit, "but it will be submission. I shall endure it as a self-mortification in order that you may all be pleased. I would rather please you than myself but still I would have it understood by all the church that I endure it as a penance for your sake."

The service was not held, and Spurgeon was not ordained. Shortly afterward, he preached on the minister's true ordination. His text: "Son of Man, I have made thee a watchman unto the house of Israel; therefore hear the word of my mouth and give them warning from me."

Spurgeon was never happy being addressed as "the Reverend" or "Pastor." Several leading Nonconformist ministers followed his lead, notably Dr. R. W. Dale and Charles Vince.

When he came to London, the traditional garb of the Nonconformist minister was a long black frock coat, a high stock with a white cravat, and a silk top hat. Spurgeon soon discarded the traditional clothes, wearing a short frock coat—almost a jacket—with an open vest, turned-down collar, and small black bow. His hat was soft felt, approaching the Trilby shape. This "rebel's" dress, which brought a storm of criticism, became the recognized uniform of Free Church ministers.

Perhaps the greatest innovation was that Spurgeon turned the pulpit into a platform. He surprised London by his utter disregard of pulpit etiquette. He adopted a direct method of address just as personal as the prophet's words when he said to the offender, "Thou art the man." Even ordinary people had no doubt about his meaning. The vague ambiguity of some preachers, which could yield half a dozen interpretations, gave way to an inescapable pointedness.

New Park Street Chapel was too small for the crowds anxious to hear the new voice. The road was blocked each Sunday, and church officers considered expansion. Meanwhile, Exeter Hall in the Strand was used for Sunday services. Even that spacious facility was not large enough, and since it was available only briefly, the officers were in a serious dilemma. The only place available was the Music Hall in the Royal Surrey Gardens. It could seat more than ten thousand people—but London knew nothing of religious services in places of popular entertainment. Immediately critics and caricaturists attacked the preacher on the mere suggestion of holding services in a music hall.

He was not deterred. The news went around that, on October 17, Spurgeon would be before the floodlights.

It was a terrible ordeal. When the preacher got to the side entrance he found the building packed from floor to ceiling, with thousands of people still unable to get inside. Some days before, Spurgeon and William Olney had gone over the building and expressed mutual fear that it was too large and the adventure almost too hazardous. Nothing like it ever had been attempted; the great audiences of Wesley and Whitefield had been in the open air. But Spurgeon and Olney were encouraged. What a triumph it would be for the gospel to be proclaimed to twelve thousand people under one roof!

The doors of the building were opened at six o'clock. Within a few minutes, there was no more room. Dr. Campbell of the *British Banner* wrote that it was "one of the most imposing, magnificent, and awful" spectacles ever seen. "No adequate idea of it can be conveyed by description; to be understood it must have been seen, and they who beheld received an impression which no time will ever obliterate."

The service began with a scripture reading and hymn. During the following prayer, something terrible happened. Suddenly there was a cry of "Fire!" In another part of the building a voice cried, "The gallery is giving way!" According to the minute book of the New Park Street Chapel:

Just after our pastor had commenced his prayer a disturbance was caused, as it is supposed, by some evil-disposed persons acting in concert, and the whole congregation was seized with a sudden panic. This caused a fearful rush to the doors, particularly from the galleries. Several persons, either in consequence of their heedless haste or from the extreme pressure of the crowd behind, were thrown down on the stone steps of the northwest staircase and were trampled on by the crowd pressing upon them. The lamentable result was that seven persons lost their lives, and twenty-eight were removed to the hospitals, seriously bruised and injured. Our pastor, not being aware that any loss of life had occurred, continued in the pulpit, endeavoring by every means in his power to alleviate the fear of the people, and was successful to a very considerable extent. In attempting to renew the service, it was found that the people were too excited to listen to him, and those who remained dispersed quietly. This lamentable circumstance produced very serious effects on the nervous system of our pastor. He was entirely prostrated for some days and compelled to relinquish his preaching engagements. Through the great mercy of our Heavenly Father, he was, however, restored so as to be able to occupy the pulpit in our own chapel on Sunday, October 31, and gradually recovered his wonted health and vigor. The Lord's name be praised!

A fund was raised to assist the sufferers, and everything possible was done to comfort the mourners. Spurgeon suffered terribly. At the house of a friend at Croydon, he seemed to linger near death. Recovering gradually, he determined to return to the Music Hall. It was decided

services would be held in the Surrey Gardens—a severe test
of the preacher's power of attraction. But the result was the
same: The building was too small for those who came from
all over London—indeed, from all over the country—to
that wonderful service.

Criticism was extremely bitter. The silliest tales were not
too silly to describe the eccentricities and antics of the "pulpit mountebank." A popular little book, *Punch in the Pulpit*,
described the Surrey Gardens service. After noting the size
of the building and the sale of literature before the service,
the writer said:

> But suddenly the business of buying and selling is
> suspended, the din of conversation is hushed; some-
> thing unusual has taken place; there is whispering,
> there is the interchange of significant looks, there is
> pointing with the finger, till at length all eyes are
> directed to one particular spot, for now it is as clear
> as the noonday that my Lord This, and my Lady
> That, have taken their seats on the platform. Now
> an air of satisfaction pervades the assembly, now it
> is thought that dissent is looking up, or that some
> important event has taken place in that kingdom
> which is not of this world, and which cometh not
> with observation or with outward show.
>
> The sermon was of the seriocomic kind; it pro-
> duced smiling, tittering, and now and then a loud
> laugh. The divinity of it was more in accordance
> with the writings of Dr. Crisp or of Dr. Hawker
> than with the writings of the New Testament. In-
> deed, in many respects, the sermon was, I think, in
> direct opposition to our Lord's Sermon on the
> Mount. The preacher of the music hall often speaks

with approbation of those who are considered to be Antonomian divines. I will not, however, deny that on this occasion there was the pleasing and energetic utterance of many good things; but, on the whole, it seemed only a semireligious service, highly gratifying to those who thirst after excitement as the drunkard thirsts after brandy or gin. I felt that pathos was wanting, that reverence was wanting, and that almost everything was wanting to make the music hall the house of God and the gate of heaven.

I was very much struck with the resemblance between the preacher of the Surrey Gardens and the preacher of the Surrey Tabernacle. It is true that one is in the morning of life, and the other is in the evening of life. The voice of one is clear as a bell, and the voice of the other is husky as a bagpipe. It is also true that one nicknames the other a "duty-faith" man and calls "duty-faith" one of the mysteries of hell. But with these exceptions, the resemblance between them is very striking. I believe that both are kind and amiable men, and that in this respect they rise above their creed. Both belong to the Hyper school, where arrogance is always exhibited, and humility is seldom taught. Both have some gold but also a more than usual quantity of brass. Both deal very largely in that mawkish thing called spiritualizing.

The Reverend C. W. Banks, in his little paper the *Earthen Vessel*, published a detailed criticism. After some words of praise, Banks wrote:

What is he doing? Whose servant is he? What proof does he give that instrumentally his is a heart-searching, a Christ-exalting, truth-unfolding, sinner-converting, church-feeding, soul-saving ministry? This is the point at issue with many whom we know, a point which we should rejoice to see clearly settled in the best sense and demonstrated beyond a doubt in the confidence of all the true churches of Christ in Christendom.

In a later issue of the *Earthen Vessel*, a communication signed "Job," believed to be the Reverend James Wells, said Spurgeon was converted at age fifteen, and added:

Heaven grant it may prove to be so for the young man's sake and that of others also! But I have, most solemnly have, my doubts as to the divine reality of his conversion.

Spurgeon's doctrine did not suit Wells and the High Calvinists, who would have nothing to do with him. Wells declared that "Spurgeon preaches all doctrine and no doctrine; all experience, and therefore no experience."

The religious press did its best to ignore Spurgeon. But to the credit of the secular journals, a number of them were fair and accurate in their reports.

Sketches caricaturing Spurgeon became popular. Stories were told of Spurgeon sliding down the handrail of the pulpit stairs at New Park Street. Told in vivid detail, they had only one fault: The pulpit at New Park Street had no stairs.

Spurgeon wrote:

Friends who inquire about silly tales may save themselves the trouble. We have been enabled in our ministry and in our walk before God so to act through grace that we have given no occasion for the slanderers, save only that we have kept the faith and been very jealous for the Lord God of Israel. Many of the stories still retailed everywhere are the very same libels which were repeated concerning Rowland Hill and others who have long gone to their rest.

Undoubtedly the preacher acted his subject. He could not do otherwise. The *Evening Star* reported:

There never yet was a popular orator who did not talk more and better with his arms than with his tongue. Mr. Spurgeon knows this instinctively. When he has read his text he does not fasten his eyes on the manuscript and his hands to a cushion; as soon as he begins he speaks and begins to act, and that not as if declaiming on the stage but as if conversing with you in the street. He seems to shake hands all round and put everyone at his ease.

The Surrey Gardens services enormously increased Spurgeon's popularity. Each Sunday morning, London was amazed to see crowds flocking to the Music Hall to hear the teenage preacher. Writing of the period, Spurgeon said:

God was with us in mighty power; conversions were numerous and some of them were of a striking kind, and all along through the years we worshiped at the music hall, there were perpetual discoveries of fresh workers, continued accessions to the church, and constant initiations of new enterprise. The college, orphanage, colportage, college missions, and all our

*various branch mission stations have followed upon
the advance made by the church during these services. We have seen good brought out of evil, and in
our case we have been made to say with David,
"Thou caused men to ride over our heads. We went
through fire and through water but Thou broughtest
us out into a wealthy place."*

The services at the Music Hall ended in 1859 when
the company directors decided to have a series of Sunday
concerts. They thought the concerts would bring in more
money—but they resulted in bankruptcy. The services returned to Exeter Hall, and the congregation settled into its
temporary home in the Strand until the great tabernacle
was erected.

The approach to Exeter Hall usually was blocked on
Sunday mornings and evenings. People came from every
direction. Frequently the building was packed with three
to four thousand persons and as many more outside clam-
ored for admission. During the week, Exeter Hall—the
home of music and eloquence—was given over to concerts
and conferences but on Sundays it was the most popular
building in the city.

On July 19, 1855, Spurgeon came of age and marked
the occasion with a special sermon. A larger congregation
than usual was on hand and demanded that it be printed. It
appeared with a portrait of the preacher, looking somewhat
worn and thin. Ultimately, all the sermons preached in Exeter Hall were compiled into a volume titled *Exeter Hall Sermons*. They had an extensive circulation in many lands.

Meanwhile, certain newspapers increased their circulation by bitter attacks on the young preacher. Editors discovered that Spurgeon provided more copy than the rest of

the preachers put together. Spurgeon began to collect what he called his "museum," a full collection of newspaper critiques and caricatures. On the front page he inscribed in bold letters: "Facts, fiction, and facetiae." In later years he found much amusement in turning the pages to read a choice paragraph to his friends.

Some ministers said Spurgeon was desecrating the Sabbath with his services in public halls. Perhaps their criticism was tinged with jealousy. One fair-minded writer described the ranks of the clergy, to which he belonged:

> *Our clergy are too highly educated for the poorer classes, or rather let me say, they are the slaves of their education; they cannot shake off its form of speech. These forms are too rigid, too confined, and the clergy will not or cannot travel out of them and take up the forms of thought and speech which will suit a less educated mode of thinking and speaking.*
>
> *They lecture on Christianity as a comparative anatomist lectures on a sequelette. If this bone of the Christian religion be here, this other bone must be there, and so on till they build up the whole fleshless array of bones, and then they clasp their hands—inwardly, it is true—and cry, "There, there it is, my scheme." There is nothing personal in it; no life, no nerves.*

The same writer said of the Nonconformist churches in the metropolis:

> *There is a settled melancholy at the back of the greater number of their ministers. Most of them have never lived, some of them have not even tried*

*to live. They know little or nothing of the world-
excellent men but profoundly ignorant of any human
nature save what they find in themselves and in
their wives. How can they preach? The one thing to
preach about they do not know.*

The London Baptist Association held its annual gathering in New Park Street Chapel. The *Freeman*, getting over its shock of nerves, reported:

*Perhaps the ministers and members of the several
churches meet so often that an annual gathering is no
novelty. Perhaps the walk through London streets or
the jolt in an omnibus or cab has fewer attractions
than the Whitsuntide jaunt by railroad or pleasant
country lane, or perhaps the thing has escaped due
attention amid the throng of metropolitan claims.
But certain it is that the London Particular Baptist
Association, holding as it does from a sense of duty a
meeting every year, has only given generally the impression of being a somewhat dull affair. Indeed, it is
not enlivening either to preacher or hearer to find
oneself in New Park Street Chapel with a congregation of seventy people on a weekday afternoon.*

*This year we are bound to say all was different.
The popularity of the Rev. C. H. Spurgeon, the re-
cently settled pastor at New Park Street, attracted a
crowded audience.*

The reporter referred to the vigor and originality of Spurgeon's sermon, noting, "These powers with due culture may by the divine blessing greatly and usefully serve the church in days to come."

The Strict Baptists returned to their criticism. They would not even allow the certainty that Spurgeon was a Christian, to say nothing of his being a Calvinist.

But still the crowds came. Spurgeon playfully wrote to his brother James:

> *Congregations more than immense. Received this year into membership in three months more than eighty; thirty more proposed for next month. The devil is wide awake but so too is our Master. The lord mayor, though a Jew, has been to the chapel. He came up to my vestry to thank me. I am going to see him at the Mansion House. Chief commissioner of police also came and paid me a visit in the vestry. But, better still, some thieves, thimbleriggers, harlots, and others have come, and some are now in the church, as also a right honorable hot-potato man, who is prominently known as a "hot-Spurgeonite."*

Spurgeon traveled up and down the country and made one or two visits abroad. He was a child of nature. Nothing pleased him more than taking two or three friends on a jaunt through rural lanes. He delighted in the open landscape, plowed fields, and healthy brown earth. The fragrance of hay was better to him than the perfume of a lady's handkerchief.

He conducted many services outside London. He was particularly happy when surrounded by a rustic crowd while he told of the glories of the Master.

In the summer of 1857 more than three thousand people assembled at the little village of Mewbourn, a few miles from Cambridge. The lonely place had never been so busy. Triumphal arches of evergreens and flowers were prepared in welcome. Shops displayed bunting, and cottages put out their flags. When the day arrived, the weather was perfect. Carriages and carts were drawn close up and wedged among the people. Many waited for hours.

Before announcing a hymn, Spurgeon said, "I think our friends will do well to take the horses out of the carriages. We cannot edify the horses but the carriages will be a great comfort to the occupants."

This was done. The preacher in a full, clear voice prayed for those present, their homes, their children, and their elderly relations. Every heart seemed touched.

After the service a meadow was cleared and tea served to about eleven hundred people who had traveled too far to return home for a meal. Then another crowd came, and Spurgeon preached again.

In the opinion of some, the largest service under one roof was at the Crystal Palace. On October 7, 1857, designated a day of humiliation and prayer because of the Indian Mutiny, trains stopped running at seven thirty in the morning. By noon a large congregation had assembled. The pulpit was erected in the northeast corner of the transept. Competent critics vowed more than twenty-five thousand people were present and could hear the preacher's voice without undue strain.

It was said that the day before the service, Spurgeon went with a friend to try the acoustics of the building. He announced the text. It was heard by a workman on the building, who claimed in later years it was through that text that he came to know the Lord.

Spurgeon made great appeals for the widows and orphans of those who died in the mutiny. There was a hearty response; more than six hundred pounds was contributed in one collection.

The secular press became more friendly. They recognized the young preacher's great gifts and absolute sincerity.

The religious press was not so kind. They continued their criticism of the places where the services were held and the dangers of such large congregations. On one occasion Spurgeon, no doubt thinking of his critics, prayed, "Wherever people are assembled to worship God, that place is sacred. Whether beneath the magnificent canopy of the blue sky or in a building such as that in which we are now assembled, every place is sacred when devoted to such a purpose, for Thou, God, art everywhere. May God be in our midst at this time, and let nothing frighten His sheep, and grant that they may feed in quietness."

The demands on his time became heavy. There were calls from all over the country for special services. Wherever he went to preach, the collection was equally divided, with half going to the fund for building a new tabernacle in London.

At his grandfather's request, he agreed to preach in connection with the Congregational Church at Stambourne. It was the old man's ministerial jubilee. The crowds were great, and the ladies were very busy making tea. The elderly man was overwhelmed with joy and listened to his grandson with deep emotion. Sometimes there would be an interruption or two, as with Whitefield and Wesley but Spurgeon was alert and very quick with repartee, so the interrupter usually was satisfied with one reply.

Thomas Olney—the "Father Olney" of New Park Street—was anxious for the pastor to preach at Tring, the little Hertfordshire town where Olney was born. It was not easy to arrange for one of the three Baptist churches to allow the use of the building for a service. The minister of one thought Spurgeon was too high in doctrine and refused.

Another declined on the ground that Spurgeon was not a sound Calvinist. But the third chapel, where William Skelton was pastor, would take a chance on Spurgeon's orthodoxy.

The place was very crowded. The minister was present, and Spurgeon noted that his suit was shiny from wear. At the close of the service he astonished the people by saying, "Now, dear friends, I have preached to you as well as I could. I don't want anything from you for myself but I note that the minister of the chapel might not object to a new suit of clothes. Father Olney down there"—he pointed to the deacon—"will give half a sovereign. I will give the same amount, and now you must give the rest."

More than one suit was provided by the collection.

Spurgeon's popularity grew by leaps and bounds after the accident at the Surrey Gardens. There were no buildings in London large enough to accommodate those who tramped from far and near to hear his voice. One paper reported:

He owes nothing to the pomp and circumstance of priesthood. There the youthful preacher stands in all the simplicity of his unsophisticated character. He owes nothing to relation or rank or the accidents of life which have sometimes contributed to great temporary popularity. What, then, is the source of this unprecedented attraction? It lies partly but not merely in the externals of his eloquence; it is primarily in the soul of the man, a soul large, liberal, and loving, a soul stamped by the characteristics of a little child while putting forth the powers of one of David's mighty men. He is one of a favored class, few in number but great in importance.

In June 1859, a violent thunderstorm passed over the

south of London. A tree on Clapham Common was struck by lightning and a man killed. Spurgeon saw an opportunity for impressing people with the solemnity of the occasion. He announced he would preach on the very spot.

Ten thousand people were said to be present there Sunday, July 10. Spurgeon used a wagon for a pulpit and preached a powerful, searching sermon on the text, "Be ye also ready." A collection was taken for the widow and her four children.

Each week, he occupied London pulpits of different denominations.

There were rumors of an enormous tabernacle to be erected for the young preacher. It was said he wanted to modernize the praise part of the service, that he was likely to bring out a new hymnal, and that he himself had written some of the hymns.

When asked how he secured such vast congregations, Spurgeon said, "I did not seek them. They have always sought me. My concern has been to preach Christ and leave the rest to His keeping."

During a typical week in 1856, his engagements included:

> *Sabbath, morning and evening, New Park Street; afternoon, address to the schools. Monday morning at Howard Hinton's chapel; afternoon, New Park Street; evening, prayer meeting. Tuesday, afternoon and evening, Leighton. Wednesday, morning and evening, Zion Chapel, Whitechapel. Thursday morning, Dalston; evening, service New Park Street. Friday morning, Dr. Fletcher's chapel; evening, Dr. Roger's chapel, Brixton.*

Spurgeon was touching all classes of the community, including many who had no religious influence. He could not have obtained such a result had he been simply a preacher of the Calvinist doctrine. He was supremely an evangelist. His great mission was to bring people to allegiance to Jesus Christ as their leader and Lord. He was a life changer, and in this mighty work he stood alone among those of his time—perhaps among those of any time.

He appealed to both educated and uneducated listeners. Even some newspapermen were drawn by the preacher in a way that would have been impossible had he not been a physician of souls able to prescribe for the rich and the poor, the cultured and the ignorant. The Reverend Jonathan Whittemore of Ainsford, editor of the *Baptist Messenger*, not only confessed his indebtedness to Spurgeon but sought his literary assistance, which readily was given. They remained friends until Whittemore's death.

Those who were in closest touch saw the martyr side of Spurgeon. While portrayed as a fearless orator, keen controversialist, and persistent dogmatist, he was almost childishly sensitive. He was very grateful for a genuine word of appreciation. To know that someone had been truly helped by his sermon would bring tears to his eyes.

There was also a subtle quality of sympathy. The suffering and sorrows of others became his own experiences. He literally had a talent for suffering—a rare gift among strong men. He was as tender to the bereaved as a mother to her hurt, small child. He often broke down at hearing of another's grief.

Most of his career was lived with physical pain. He bravely endured his cross and made his suffering comfort and strengthen others. In later years he would sit heavily in his chair in the private room—"the guv'nor's room"—at the college. As he talked, leaning hard on his stick, every breath seemed drawn in pain.

"The enemy has me today," he once said, "in both knees. I am afraid I cannot walk to the platform." He straightened himself as well as he could, tightened his lips, and, with the aid of an arm on one side and his stick on the other, managed to get along the corridor and into the college room, where the rafters rang with the welcome of 125 students. A little more erect, he got to the platform and took his seat. Then the enemy gave him another twinge. His face was drawn for a moment but when he looked up, a new light in his eye, he said, "God gives to some a talent for suffering."

That afternoon many men felt ashamed they had ever spoken of their paltry aches and pains. They had seen a great soul endure physical agony with the radiance of the Almighty.

SEVEN

Early and late in life, Spurgeon gloried in his belief in Calvinism. In the first sermon preached in the Metropolitan Tabernacle, he said, "I am not ashamed to avow myself a Calvinist, although I claim to be rather a Calvinist according to Calvin than after the modern, debased fashion. I do not hesitate to take the name of Baptist. You have here"—he pointed to the open baptistery—"substantial evidence that I am not ashamed of that ordinance of our Lord Jesus Christ but if I am asked to say what is my creed, I think I must reply, 'It is Jesus Christ.' My venerated predecessor, Dr. Gill, has left a body of divinity admirable and excellent in its way but the body of divinity to which I would pin and bind myself forever, God helping me, is not his system of divinity or any other human treatise but Jesus Christ, who is the sum and substance of the gospel, who is in Himself all theology, the Incarnation of every precious truth, the all-glorious embodiment of the Way, the Truth, and the Life."

The Calvinists of Spurgeon's day were mainly of the Hyper-Calvinist school, with Calvin's grim logic but not his human sympathy. Spurgeon did not set out to be a theologian but those who knew him recognized his wide reading in theology and his intimate acquaintance with the Puritans. Probably his collection of Puritan literature was by far the most extensive owned by an individual.

Robertson Nicoll recalled of Spurgeon:

There are many things in his sermons which show that he was not at all the narrow and illiterate bigot that many people think him; on the contrary he had a great breadth of mind; he made serious concessions to the new spirit and was far better read and far more able and powerful intellectually than most people knew.

Spurgeon's theology, as all general theology, takes its flavor from the individual's temperament and outlook. Spurgeon was different from Augustine and Calvin. He had the warm imagination of a poet and the passionate affection of a great lover, with an unsurpassed gift of rhetoric.

In 1536 John Calvin, a young Frenchman of twenty-seven seeking religious liberty, passed through Geneva, where Farel was preaching the Reformation. Calvin was persuaded to join the work. Because of their zeal, they were expelled from the city. Calvin returned in 1541 and "proceeded to govern [the city] as though he were not sure whether he was in charge of a university or a reformatory."

"The Laws and Statutes of Geneva," which Calvin formulated, cover almost all matters of life and conduct, from prohibiting baggy trousers and long hair to polite forms of address and the banning of naughty words. Calvin set up a consistory, an ecclesiastical court to supervise morals and manners. He provided adequate housing for students. The university at Geneva developed rapidly and became famous throughout Europe as a cultural center for Protestants of all lands.

Calvin's doctrine was that of the Reformers. He preached the Bible as the Word of God, the sole authority for humans. No priest is needed as mediator; the human's conscience, directed by God, must be the judge of all actions. Calvin applied his principles to matters besides religion, teaching that no obedience should be given to church or state that is not first sanctioned by conscience.

The principles governing Geneva spread widely with the fires of the Reformation, affecting the destinies of Holland, Scotland, and New England. Geneva prospered and became a beacon.

After twenty-three years of incessant toil and suffering, Calvin died at age fifty-five. Geneva—chosen by nations of all faiths as their common ground—is his lasting monument.

But Calvin is remembered not for his love of learning and his passion to make education the birthright of every child, not for his advanced ideas of civil government, not for his amazing writings and commentaries on the Bible, not for his widely admired book, *The Institutes of the Christian Religion*. He is remembered for the burning of the heretic Michael Servetus and the dark chapter of his theology dealing with predestination.

Spurgeon preached in Calvin's pulpit in connection with an international thanksgiving service. He received the Medal of Remembrance. He rejoiced in Calvin's practical work. As he said, Geneva in Calvin's day was a city of refuge. A colony of strangers acknowledging no allegiance found a congenial atmosphere there in which to live and study. Exiles for conscience's sake were more than welcome; they came from the ends of the earth, and as long as they kept within the limits of the law, they were protected.

Yet Calvin cannot escape the shadow of Servetus.

Spurgeon loved the many-sidedness of the man. Even in his serious *Institutes*, Calvin found space for lively, entertaining paragraphs. Describing how God appears in human form, Calvin said, "Who of the meanest capacity understands not that God lisps as it were with us, just as nurses are accustomed to speak to infants." On the guidance of scripture: ". . .The scripture, collecting in our minds the otherwise confused notions of Deity, dispels the darkness and gives us a clearer view of the true God."

Calvin's doctrines of election and reprobation have become a nightmare to many and a cause of controversy from the time they were introduced. Calvin himself thought they were terrible. Augustine and others had taught a doctrine of predestination and the absolute sovereignty of God over His universe but most of them had hesitated to go to the end of the logical process. Calvin, not a man to stay in intellectual halfway houses, proceeded. He wrote:

> *Predestination we call the eternal decree of God, by which He hath determined in Himself what He would have to become of every individual of mankind. For they are not all created with a similar destiny; but eternal life is foreordained for some and eternal damnation for others. We assert that by an eternal and immutable counsel, God hath once for all determined, both whom He would admit to salvation and whom He would condemn to destruction.*

Calvin was trained in the law, and his theology bears the marks of legal training. He pushed the case for the prosecution relentlessly to get a verdict, even though the verdict seemed an outrage. It is a strange paradox that the doctrine of divine sovereignty has produced heroes and given them courage as no other teaching has done.

In Spurgeon's day, Calvinist preachers dwelt largely on predestination and reprobation, almost ignoring Calvin's other proclamations. They did him a great injustice by their omissions. Systems of theology must be judged not by selecting one dogma and viewing it out of relation to the whole but by honestly endeavoring to see the entire scheme, noting how one doctrine limits, extends, or qualifies another.

Father Simon, a well-known Roman Catholic priest, wrote of Calvin:

> *As Calvin was endued with a lofty genius, we are constantly meeting with something in his commentaries which delights the mind, and in consequence of his intimate and perfect acquaintance with human nature, his ethics are truly charming, while he does his utmost to maintain their accordance with the sacred text.*

Many theologians encouraged their pupils to read Calvin's works. Spurgeon quoted Calvin frequently and insisted he himself was a Calvinist but did not blindly follow the great Genevan. Spurgeon shrewdly saw the limits beyond which no interpreter could advance safely.

Spurgeon's nearest neighbor was the Reverend James Wells, a High Calvinist leader whose references to Spurgeon were often rude. With enjoyment and skill, he attacked Spurgeon's departure from true Calvinism. Sometimes

Spurgeon replied in kind. In a lecture to his students on sermons, Spurgeon said:

> *Do not rehearse five or six doctrines with unvarying*
> *monotony of repetition. Buy a theological barrel*
> *organ, brethren, with five tunes accurately adjusted,*
> *and you will be qualified to practice as an ultra-*
> *Calvinistic preacher at Zoar or at Jireh, if you also*
> *purchase at some vinegar factory a good supply of*
> *bitter, acrid abuse of Arminians, and duty-faith*
> *men. Brains and grace are optional but the organ*
> *and the wormwood are indispensable. It is ours to*
> *perceive and rejoice in a wider range of truth. All*
> *that these good men hold of grace and sovereignty we*
> *maintain as firmly and boldly as they; but we dare*
> *not shut our eyes to other teachings of the Word, and*
> *we feel bound to make full proof of our ministry by*
> *declaring the whole counsel of God.*

Spurgeon's theology was like marble strata running in different directions. It reflected the time in which he lived as well as his genius. He followed the main outline of Calvin. He read Calvin's *Institutes* but rarely quoted from it. He sometimes turned to the bright side of Jonathan Edwards, the New England theologian. Spurgeon's Calvinism was shot through with his own type of religion and resulted in the sterner doctrines being interpreted with the tenderness of mysticism. He believed God is first and last, and everything depends on divine will—but the will of God is to reveal the love of God. Spurgeon loved to talk of the all-pervading grace that came through Jesus Christ, and the love of the Father that never lost its freshness.

Small minds strive for a clear-cut system in which all

mysteries can be reduced to harmony. Spurgeon, on the other hand, was not greatly concerned with harmonizing his theology. He recognized the difference between theology and religion. The controversy between Calvinists and Arminians, he wrote, "is exceedingly important but it does not so involve the vital point of personal godliness as to make eternal life dependent upon our holding either system of theology."

Spurgeon saw that in theology, as in life, are problems we cannot solve. Quoting Deuteronomy 29:29: "The secret things belong unto the LORD our God: but those things which are revealed belong unto us and to our children for ever, that we may do all the words of this law."

That verse practically covered the main outline of Spurgeon's theology. In life we constantly come to roads marked "Private." Curiosity, the mother of learning, prompts us to explore the paths but at the end of the road is the closed door, the barred gate, the cul-de-sac. God has kept some things to Himself, and, at least in this life, they are not made known to His children.

Calvinism leaves room for mysticism. It does not attempt to explain away the great mysteries. Truth, as we know it, does not form a perfect circle but seems to lie in parallel lines that never meet.

The sovereignty of God and the Fatherhood of God are equally clear in the scriptures. How far does the doctrine of the Fatherhood of God extend? Calvin declared that it stretches as far as His sovereignty. By virtue of creation, humans are children of God and enter the family of God through faith in Jesus Christ. Romans 8:15: "For ye have not received the spirit of bondage again to fear; but ye have received the Spirit of adoption, whereby we cry, Abba, Father."

According to Calvinism, there are three stages in our

human kinship to God. We are His children by creation and as such are the objects of His love. Secondly, we are His children by redemption, and thirdly, by the adoption and sanctification of the Holy Spirit. Spurgeon loved to dwell on the relationship of the believer to God in Jesus Christ. If one wishes to know the wonders of divine love in communion with the Father, Spurgeon is a valuable instructor.

In contrast are a number of doctrines which are difficult to harmonize. Calvinism has been much criticized because of the tenets of election and the Covenant, yet Calvin stated them in the words of the scriptures. Calvin's teaching about the depravity of human nature, if it stood alone, would be one of the most terrible chapters in literature. Humans are totally depraved; human nature works in opposition to God's will. But standing in antithesis is the grace of God, sovereign and free, abundant and irresistible. Just as a subtle, strange healing power begins to work in us wherever a physical wound occurs, grace contains the active mercy of God, from everlasting to everlasting.

Spurgeon delighted in the doctrine of grace. In his view, it had no limits. Like the sun, it was made to rise on the evil and the good, and it should lead us to acknowledge God in Christ. Spurgeon found peace for his heart and rest for his mind in recognizing it was not his duty to bring into harmony the vast body of truth found in the scriptures.

With an eye for the practical, Spurgeon related his theology to the needs of the people. He once told students:

> Do not make minor doctrines main points. For instance, the great problems of sublapsarianism and superlapsarianism, the trenchant debates concerning eternal filiation, the earnest dispute concerning the double procession, and the pre- or post-millenarian

*schemes, however important some may deem them,
are practically of very little concern to that godly
widow woman, with seven children to support by
her needle, who wants far more to hear of the loving-
kindness of God or Providence than of these mysteries profound. If you preach to her on the faithfulness
of God to His people, she will be cheered and helped
in the battle of life. But difficult questions will per-
plex her or send her to sleep. She is, however, the type
of hundreds of those who most require your care. Our
great master theme is the good news from heaven;
the tidings of mercy through the atoning death of
Jesus, mercy to the chief of sinners upon their believing in Jesus.*

Spurgeon believed it was better to unveil the glory of
God in the face of Jesus Christ than to solve problems of
scriptural harmony. He recognized no knowledge of God
except through the scriptures. His idea of the spiritual use
of the Bible placed it beyond the scope of historical criticism. He would say, "It is not for us to sit in judgment
upon the Word but to let the Word judge us."

There are three basic principles of religious authority:
the Rationalist, the Medieval, and the Reformed. They depend, respectively, on human reason, the utterance of the
church, and the words of scripture.

All agree God is the absolute authority but God may
have been silent. Latter-day paganism adopted the old
view that the Creator had not spoken, and if He had, the
human mind was insufficient to receive His message.

If, on the other hand, it is believed God has spoken
and revealed Himself to humans, the question arises, "Is
there any record of the revelation?" Humans clearly cannot

find God by searching. It is equally clear the Almighty could make Himself known to us if He desires. Has He not done so?

Spurgeon's answer was emphatic. He accepted the Bible as the supreme authority in all matters of faith and practice. The church could be only a source of authority in making known the knowledge of God; human intelligence, however brilliant its theorizing might be, can never be an authority.

Spurgeon held that in the scriptures God had stated all that was necessary for salvation and right living. The proof of the scriptures is the witness of the Holy Spirit in the believer. When received sincerely, the Truth carries its own illumination. All through his life, Spurgeon took the Bible's promises at their face value and used them in prayer and preaching. He found great comfort and delight in them. To Spurgeon it would have been as silly to question the promises of the New Testament as to question the value of sunlight. He lived in its radiance.

The stern truth of the Calvinist faith was held practically by all Protestants. They might have expressed their faith in the "Articles of Belief of the Church of England." These models of Calvinist doctrine were accepted without question.

Spurgeon, with the evangelicals, believed it was a terrible thing to fall into the hands of the living God. He preached the doctrine of eternal punishment. It gripped his heart and frequently moved his conscience. It was the practice of the age for preachers to try to frighten people into ways of goodness but that was not Spurgeon's method. When he preached the stern truth, it was with tears. He insisted there was no reason why any soul should be lost; whoever would trust Christ would be saved.

He loved to linger over the tender aspects of the gospel. He delighted in proclaiming the doctrine of the cross. Calvary filled his soul with wonder and his speech with eloquence.

In Spurgeon's time, some Calvinist preachers out-Calvined Calvin. They were not content with his stern representation of God's sovereignty. They insisted all God did was of His own will, for His own glory. Grace was undeserved and had nothing to do with any thought of justice the creature might ask of the Lord of the world.

Spurgeon, meanwhile, made God's love, revealed in Christ's mercy, the center of his teaching. In a sermon at Exeter Hall on "Plenteous Redemption," he defined his doctrine of election:

> *Christ has redeemed the souls of all His people who shall ultimately be saved. To state it after the Calvinistic fashion, Christ has redeemed His elect. But since you do not know His elect until they are revealed, we will alter that and say, Christ has redeemed all penitent souls; Christ has redeemed all believing souls and Christ has redeemed the souls of all those who die in infancy, seeing it is to be received, that all those who die in infancy are written in the Lamb's Book of Life and are graciously privileged by God to go at once to heaven instead of toiling through this weary world. The souls of all those who were written before all worlds in the Lamb's Book of Life, who in process of time are humbled before God, who in due course are led to lay hold of Christ Jesus as the only refuge of their souls, who hold on their way, and ultimately attain to heaven—these, I believe, were redeemed, and I most firmly*

and solemnly believe the souls of none other men
were in that sense subjects of redemption.

Theoretically, there were limits to redemption but practically, the barriers were all taken down. Spurgeon's doctrine was: Whoever will, let him come. Other preachers ingeniously created limits and restrictions but Spurgeon saw God's mercy to be as wide as the sea.

Spurgeon's doctrine of the church was that of the *ecclesia*: the "called out," who are born again through faith in Jesus Christ. He had no doctrine of unregenerate church membership, nor did he admit there was any place in church fellowship for babes unconscious of belief. He preached individual responsibility: Humans are saved or lost according to their relationship to Jesus. The responsibility placed on the saved individual leads to the doctrine of personal holiness and progressive sanctification. The redeemed are not passive but active agents, working together with God.

Spurgeon rejected what he called a "duty-faith salvation" and insisted on the duty of the faithful to follow the Lord's example in doing good. For him, the raw material of religion was: "Trust in the Lord and do good." He had both sanctified common sense and shrewd worldly wisdom. He did not withdraw from the world any more than the Good Samaritan withdrew from the thieves' victim.

EIGHT

In June 1856, a committee was appointed to consider building a new place of worship for New Park Street, at an estimated cost of at least thirty-one thousand pounds. A church meeting was held and resolutions passed unanimously that a tabernacle to seat five thousand people be erected. Subscription lists were opened. Almost three thousand pounds were promised, and the committee members were optimistic the rest would be forthcoming quickly.

At a later meeting, Spurgeon described the work they proposed to do and the need for it:

> The Lord hath given me favor in the eyes of the people and blessed me with not a little success. The number of members has so increased as well nigh to fill this place. Indeed, we have three hundred more friends whose names are on the church book than are able to sit down in the area of the chapel to partake of the Communion.

Referring to his own position regarding expansion, Spurgeon continued:

> *Where are the crowds on the Sabbath evenings? It is my duty to look after them. Long ago I made up my mind that either a suitable place must be built, or I would resign my pastorate. . . . I would become an evangelist and turn rural dean of all the commons in England and vicar of all the hedgerows. Some nobleman, speaking of this matter, said, "Who knows whether the place will ever be built?" I wrote to him, saying, "You need not ask that question, my lord; there's a man alive who will earn the money." Yes, it shall be had. I have prayed to the Lord and shall keep on praying, and He will not refuse my request.*

It was not easy to select the site. A comparatively quiet neighborhood was needed, free from the bustle of the city. The committee decided on Newington, at a spot near the Elephant and Castle, a coach station which was a popular stop for refreshment. Newington was originally "New Town," an outlying district of Southwark. In those years it was not uncommon to see sheep and cows from a nearby farm being driven down the road. The streets eventually would become crowded as London took in the suburbs of Newington, Camberwell, Stockwell, and Clapham.

All London seemed interested in the new, immense building; it was one of the wonders of the time. Early in the morning on the day of the stone laying, a prayer meeting was held. Crowds blocked the decorated roads, where laurel leaves were used for triumphal arches. A streamer announced, YOU ARE TRULY WELCOME.

It must have been a great day for Spurgeon. He had been in London only a few years, and he was acclaimed as the most popular preacher, probably the most popular man, in the country. But he had not forgotten the voice he had heard: "Seekest thou great things for thyself? Seek them not."

Sir Morton Peto occupied the place of honor; Spurgeon's father took part in the ceremony. One of the officers read a short history of the church, eliciting frequent cheers. But what the crowd waited to hear was Spurgeon's address, and they were not disappointed. He placed under the foundation stone a bottle containing a Bible, the Baptist Confession of Faith signed by Benjamin Keach, a declaration by the deacons, Dr. Rippon's hymnbook, and a program of the service.

Spurgeon said the building was to be "a Grecian place of worship." He explained:

It seemed to me that there are two sacred languages in the world: There was the Hebrew of old. There is only one other sacred language, the Greek, which is very dear to every Christian heart. Every Baptist place should be Grecian, never Gothic.

Referring to the denominational character of the building, he declared:

We have one Lord, one faith, one baptism, and dear to our hearts is that Word, the communion of saints. Whosoever loves the Lord Jesus Christ in the spirit and in truth has a heart welcome to communion with the church of Christ. I see around us Independent brethren. I see also a Strict Communion brother, and he will address you. I have some of my dearest friends, ministers of the Church of England, and I glory in the fact that, however firmly a man may hold the truth, he can give his hand to every man that loves Jesus Christ.

There was predictable criticism. Several daily papers charged that it was simply an exhibition of colossal vanity. Who was Spurgeon to imagine he could sustain a congregation of five thousand people from Sunday to Sunday? No one had ever attempted such a foolhardy undertaking. Whitefield and Wesley had drawn great congregations but not regularly in the same place; they had been wise enough to pitch their tents in different parts of the country. Geographically, for anyone to leave the metropolis and build such a structure at Newington was simply courting disaster.

Some of the critics were philosophical, others theological, all venomous. A clerical friend wrote:

A monster chapel is in the same category with a monster ship, a monster newspaper, or a monster bell. All monsters are expensive. Nature or art goes out of its way to produce them, and we must go out of our way to maintain them; and what expenses does a chapel of gigantic dimensions necessarily involve, and what questionable expedients are resorted to for meeting those expenses! Many of them will not bear the light unless we can believe that the gospel may be made use of for getting architectural magnificence or any object of mere world ambition.

It was suggested that this kind of building would be a "vortex," drawing people of other churches as well as the unchurched. There was fear of what might happen. There could be scenes of mass panic. But the most interesting objection was raised by Mr. Jay:

> *The practice of preaching three times on the Lord's Day was the devil's invention for killing ministers but what is that compared with the labor of preaching several times a week to an overwhelming multitude? No man can afford to do this, and God never qualified a man to do this, and no principle of religion and no necessities of the church require him to do this.*
>
> *Here is a young man nearly overpowered with exertions in preaching to immense multitudes. Suggestions have been made that he shall go on the Continent to recruit his exhausted strength, and already there are rumors of a great meeting to welcome him back. This is just as reasonable as it would be to give a bowl of brandy and water to a convalescent who had previously injured his health by drinking of that deleterious compound.*

But Spurgeon went on with the great project, and friends from all over the world came to his aid. Amid the media's predictions that the money for the tabernacle would never be raised, a friend came to Spurgeon with a request that they go for a drive. He then inquired the cost of the building. Spurgeon told him they would need about another twenty thousand pounds. His friend said, "I want to save you from anxiety. I shall place securities for twenty thousand pounds to your account, and you will use whatever you require so that the building may be opened free of debt."

When the time came, Spurgeon accepted a donation of fifty pounds from his generous friend. They must have been greatly amused to read the tirades of the critics.

After a brief rest, Spurgeon began preaching tours with renewed zest. Half the offerings were given to the new building, half to the local church. The offerings amounted to several thousand pounds, of which the preacher received nothing. It frequently was reported that Spurgeon was making a fortune from his preaching, that he had a sizable home with many servants and a carriage. It was rumored a magnificent fortune had been left to him.

The reports gained such credibility that at the stone laying of the tabernacle, Spurgeon referred to them:

> *I approve of ministers having a good salary for preaching, and in this respect I would cordially say that I am for my own part perfectly satisfied but if anyone should leave ministers a large sum of money, they generally lose their voice or get an attack of bronchitis or something of that sort that puts an end to their preaching.*

About this time, something happened that affected Spurgeon's growing popularity in the United States. After the usual weeknight service at New Park Street, a fugitive slave from South Carolina, John Andrew Jackson, was introduced by Spurgeon and asked to tell of his sufferings and escape. Jackson held the congregation for an hour, finishing to passionate excitement. Spurgeon declared:

> *Slavery is the foulest blot that ever stained a national escutcheon and may have to be washed out with blood. America is in many respects a glorious country but it may be necessary to teach her some wholesome lessons at the point of the bayonet, to*

*carve freedom into her with the bowie knife or send
it home to her heart with revolvers. Better far should
it come to this issue, that North and South should be
rent asunder, and the states of the Union shivered
into a thousand fragments, than that slavery should
be suffered to continue.*

*Some American divines seem to regard it, indeed,
with wonderful complacency. They so have accustomed
themselves to wrap it up in soft phrases that they lose
sight of its real character. They call it a "peculiar institution," until they forget in what its peculiarity con-
sists. It is, indeed, a peculiar institution, just as the
devil is a peculiar angel and as hell is a peculiarly hot
place. For my part, I hold such miserable tampering
with sin in abhorrence and can hold no communion of
any sort with those who are guilty of it.*

Many attempts were made to get Spurgeon to tone
down his statements. He was advised the printed sermon
would lose its American circulation, and no further help
would be forthcoming from across the Atlantic. This was
true. American publishers eliminated all references to slavery.
Spurgeon subsequently declared in a stinging letter to
the *Watchman and Reflector*:

*I do from my inmost soul detest slavery anywhere
and everywhere, and although I commune at the
Lord's Table with men of all creeds, yet with a slave-
holder I have no fellowship of any kind or sort.
Whenever one has called upon me I have considered
it my duty to express my detestation of his wicked-
ness, and would as soon think of receiving a murderer into the church or into any sort of fellowship, as*

> *a man-stealer. Nevertheless, as I have preached in*
> *London and not in New York, I have seldom made*
> *any allusion to slavery in my sermons.*

The letter was reprinted in many American journals and resulted in a complete boycott of anything referring to Spurgeon. A Boston correspondent wrote to the *Freeman* in 1860:

> *Our Baptist papers are overflowing with indigna-*
> *tion and call on all publishers and booksellers to*
> *banish the books of our worthy young friend from*
> *their counters. . . . The poor slaveholders are at their*
> *wits' end and know not what to do to save their*
> *doomed system. The* Montgomery Mail *says: "The*
> *Vigilance Committee is engaged in burning books,*
> *and the two volumes of Spurgeon's sermons have*
> *been contributed to their bonfires, and they will be*
> *burnt."*

Spurgeon was persuaded to take a brief holiday. He happened to be at Baden-Baden in June 1860, where the Emperor Napoleon and eight other crowned heads were attending a conference. "One can hardly walk in any direction without stumbling upon a grand duke or being run over by the horses of an emperor," Spurgeon chronicled.

It was, however, impossible for Spurgeon to refrain from preaching. In almost every town he visited in Switzerland, he was asked to speak. His greatest joy was in Geneva. The historian of the Reformation, Dr. Merle d'Aubigné, took him to his home—the very house where Calvin had lived. Spurgeon accepted an invitation to preach in Calvin's pulpit. His own account is worth preserving:

I was really allowed to stand in the pulpit of John Calvin. I am not superstitious but the first time I saw the medal of John Calvin I kissed it, and when the pastors saw my reverence for him they presented me with a magnificent medal. I preached in the Cathedral of St. Peter. I do not suppose half the people understood me but it did not matter about understanding; they were very glad to sing and to join in heart with the worship.

I did not feel very comfortable when I came out in full canonicals but the request was put to me in such a beautiful way that I could have worn the Pope's tiara if they had asked me. They said, "Our dear brother comes to us from another country. Now, when an ambassador comes from another country, he has a right to wear his own costume at court but as a mark of very great esteem, he sometimes condescends to the weakness of the country which he visits and will wear court dress." "Well," I said, "Yes, that I will certainly; but I shall feel like running in a sack." It was John Calvin's cloak, and that reconciled me to it very much. I do love that man of God, suffering all his life long, not only enduring persecution from without but a complication of disorders from within and yet serving his Master with all his heart. I want to ask your prayers for the church at Geneva. That little republic stands like an island surrounded by France.

The Metropolitan Tabernacle was completed in March 1861. The architect was Pocock, the builder William Higgs, a church officer and intimate friend of the pastor. The building was 146 feet long, 81 feet wide, and 62 feet high. There were 5,500 seats of all kinds, with room for 6,000 people without overcrowding. The lecture hall accommodated 900, the schoolroom 1,000 children. There were 6 classrooms with kitchens, toilets, a ladies' meeting room, young men's classrooms, a secretary's office, three vestries, and ample storerooms.

A prayer meeting was held on March 25. A week before, more than two thousand people had attended a prayer meeting and bazaar. A large sum of money still was required if the building was to be opened free of debt, and the pastor had pledged that it would not be open unless every penny was paid.

When Spurgeon held the first service in the great tabernacle, the dream of his life was fulfilled. The building was thronged with a thousand people more than it was supposed to accommodate. The congregation included men and women of all classes and conditions.

Spurgeon's text was: "And daily in the temple and in every house they ceased not to teach and preach Jesus Christ." Evidently moved by the occasion, he began with an unfamiliar slowness of speech:

I do not know whether there are any persons here present who can contrive to put themselves into my position and to feel my present feelings. If they can effect that they will give me credit for meaning what I say when I declare that I feel totally unable to preach. Indeed, I think I should scarcely attempt a sermon but rather give a sort of declaration of the truths from which future sermons shall be made. I will give you bullion rather than coin, block from the quarry and not the statue from the chisel. It appears that the one subject upon which men preached in the apostolic age was Jesus Christ.

He traced the theme of the apostles and declared that Christ alone would be the subject of his ministry.

That evening the Reverend William Brock of Blooms-bury preached. The following night the first of the public meetings was held, with Sir Henry Havelock presiding. It was a meeting of contributors; for several hours before it began, a number of men were busy receiving and recording contributions brought by hundreds of voluntary collectors. The amounts varied from a few pennies to many pounds. Rich and poor followed each other into the treasury.

Spurgeon announced that all the money required had been received. At the close, he said:

> *My friends, I would ask you all to offer one more prayer for me. What am I to do with such a work as this? It is not the launching of the vessel; it is the keeping her afloat. Who is sufficient for these things? How shall I, a young man, a feeble child, go in and out before this people? Blessed be God, there is a glorious answer to this question. "My grace is sufficient for thee; for My strength is made perfect in weakness."*

During the rest of that week and the following week, services were held each night. Among the eminent preachers who conducted them were Dr. Winslow, the Reverend Hugh Stowell Brown, the Reverend Blomfield, and the Reverend J. A. Spurgeon. Henry Vincent delivered an oration on nonconformity that made a fitting conclusion to the wonderful series. There was no parallel to these gatherings in church history.

The amazing experiences connected with these opening services, the unprecedented sight of thousands of people walking out to Newington night after night, the huge building—all convinced the press Spurgeon was not a mountebank or charlatan. Dr. Campbell described him as:

An individual chosen for the accomplishment of a special work and mentally, morally, and physically, he is in every way admirably adapted to his mission. His seeming defects in the eye of some are special excellences. He is not to be judged by the petty rules that poor mortals have derived from the creeping experience of the past. Nothing were easier than to prove that he is often wild and erratic and transgresses the canons of the schools. He is above the schools, he is a law to himself and wholly unamenable to the tribunals of criticism. He simply exerts the powers peculiar and wonderful with which God has endowed him. He reads, he expounds, he prays, he preaches as nobody else did or probably will ever do. He is an original and a rebel in everything but his insurgency notwithstanding, he is the impersonation of profoundest loyalty to a higher law. Comets are not less amenable to rule than suns; through his disobedience he achieves his triumphs and rules the millions.

Spurgeon might well have felt overawed by the task awaiting him. The great adventure was begun, the dream come true. He had the largest place of worship in the empire's capital city. At all the opening services the crowds surged about the doors.

He must have pondered: But what of the future? Who could carry that weight?

Yet even when depressed by the magnitude of his mission, Spurgeon was strangely sure it would be fulfilled. His confidence was not in himself. Few men possessed more genuine humility. He was confident God was with him, he had not been seeking great things for himself, and his motive had been to bring honor to his Lord, to bring men and women to know his Savior.

There were times during the building of the tabernacle when his faith was sorely tried. On one occasion Spurgeon was at a ministerial luncheon when Dr. Brock asked how the funds were coming in. Spurgeon replied, "Quite well but we shall need a thousand pounds for the builder on Saturday—and the Lord will send it."

The doctor remarked, "Be careful. There is only a small margin between faith and presumption."

A few minutes later a telegram was brought in. Spurgeon read it and passed it on. The message from the church secretary read: "Thousand pounds received for new building."

Brock put down his knife and fork and said, "Brethren, I think we should rise and sing the 'Doxology'."

There is a clear distinction between conceit and confidence. Spurgeon may have had reason for vanity but those who knew him recognized his honest humility. Yet he always had the confidence that belongs to great personalities who are called, sometimes against their will, to fulfill a great destiny.

NINE

Spurgeon's college was intended for young men who had been called by God to the Baptist ministry and who had already preached acceptably for at least two years. The story of the college is an allegory of faith. Spurgeon's ministry had given Baptists a larger place in the national life. His influence had broadened the theology of the time, deepened piety, and accelerated progress. His college changed religious teaching in England.

The Pastors' College was so named either because it was for the training of pastors or—more likely—because it was the pastor's most cherished creation. Speaking of the college, Spurgeon once said, "By that I multiply myself," calling it his "firstborn and best-beloved."

The college began in stirring times. Traditional beliefs already were feeling the shock of the new views associated with Charles Darwin. The new economics, popularized by Charles Kingsley and John Ruskin, was filtering through the minds of the middle class and the more worldly working class. The Anglo-Catholic movement associated with John Henry Newman alarmed ultra-Protestants.

Spurgeon did not set out to counteract the tendency of the times but to experiment. He found among his converts several young men who were beginning to preach but whose educations were limited. The most promising included T. W. Medhurst, a true Cockney born in Bermondsey four months after Spurgeon. Medhurst had served an apprenticeship to John Porter, rope maker and deacon of East Street Baptist Chapel in Walworth. After his baptism Medhurst went once a week to study theology with Spurgeon, who then was lodging on Dover Road. After six months Medhurst began to preach and was greatly blessed in his ministry at Kingston-on-Thames, Coleraine in Ireland, Glasgow, and Portsmouth. He baptized nearly one thousand people. Clearly he was called to the ministry. Spurgeon recognized his gifts and, after Medhurst had been conducting services two years, decided to pay for his education.

The problem arose: Where could the young man be trained? It was useless to send him to existing colleges, as their entrance examinations were much too severe.

Spurgeon talked the matter over with the Reverend Jonathan George of Walworth, who suggested a meeting with the Reverend George Rogers, Congregational minister of Albany Road Chapel in Camberwell. None could have anticipated the results of that meeting. Spurgeon was greatly impressed by the obvious sincerity and solid learning of the one he afterward said was preordained of God to be the first principal of the college. In the little sitting room Spurgeon, George, Rogers, and Medhurst knelt in prayer. There, in brilliant naïveté, the Pastors' College was born.

Spurgeon wrote:

I had not even a remote idea of whereunto it would grow. There were springing up around me, as my own spiritual children, many earnest young men who felt an irresistible impulse to preach the gospel, and yet with half an eye it could be seen that their lack of education would be a sad hindrance to them. It was not in my heart to bid them cease their preaching, and, had I done so, they would in all probability have ignored my recommendation. As it seemed that preach they would, though their attainments were very slender, no other course was open but to give them an opportunity to educate themselves for the work.

No college at that time appeared to me to be suitable for the class of men that Providence and the grace of God drew round me. They were mostly poor, and most of the colleges involved necessarily a considerable outlay to the student; for even where the education was free, books, clothes, and other incidental expenses required a considerable sum per annum. Moreover, it must be frankly admitted that my views of the gospel and of the mode of training preachers were and are somewhat peculiar. I may have been uncharitable in my judgment but I thought the Calvinism of the theology usually taught to be very doubtful, and the fervor of the generality of the students to be far behind their literary attainments.

The little college started on faith, with no endowments or subscriber lists. With a staff of one man, it began a work that blessed hundreds of thousands and carried the gospel literally to the ends of the earth, always maintaining its purpose as a missionary institution. Spurgeon declared that home and foreign missions were "two sides of the same penny." The Pastors' College never tried to make ministers but to help men with ministerial gifts to obtain better training for their work. It was a unique mission.

In the early days, income was provided by three people: Mr. Winsor, William Olney, and Spurgeon himself. As the work grew, increased expenses made it necessary to seek other resources.

The college supper became one popular funding source. It began in 1865 when T. R. Phillips generously resolved to give a supper in the lecture hall, at which the work of the college would be reported and the president presented with special gifts. At the first supper, 350 pounds was contributed. The second year this increased to 900 pounds. It grew steadily until contributions of more than 2,000 pounds were received each supper.

During Christmas week of 1865, a great bazaar was held at the tabernacle to secure funds for building new chapels in and around London. The bazaar opened December 26, with 1,700 people visiting the halls. Nearly 900 pounds was received in two days.

Mrs. Spurgeon's stall was a great attraction. The students had a stall to themselves. Each visitor received a letter from Spurgeon. He wrote:

> I have used my utmost to increase the number of our
> Baptist churches, and as a result solid and flourishing
> churches have been founded in Wandsworth, Stepney,
> Bromley, Redhill, and Ealing, while the small place in
> Paradise Place has become a noble house of prayer, and
> in Bermondsey a chapel is nearly completed for the use
> of a congregation now in connection with the church in
> the Metropolitan Tabernacle and worshiping in a

small room. From the success already achieved I am encouraged to attempt yet greater things.

The denominational paper, the *Freeman*, in a leading article about Baptist colleges, said:

The Baptists of Great Britain have nine colleges which are educating 264 young men with a yearly income of 13,379 pounds. It is significant and suggestive that one college receives nearly a third of these students and more than a third of these receipts. Evidently Mr. Spurgeon and his friends are more earnest and liberal in the work of providing collegiate training for the ministry than are the major part of our pastors and ministers.

Spurgeon had no intention of rivaling other colleges. He simply wanted to provide an institution to train men who would be able to present the gospel in the language of the common people. His motive was more than justified: In ten years, the college men baptized 20,676 people. The gross increase in their churches was 30,677. The students went into districts where no Free churches existed; many began their work by holding open-air services in the marketplace or on street corners.

There was no architectural beauty about the little building tucked away behind the tabernacle at the bottom of Temple Street—just three floors of red brick, with stone dressings. On the ground floor was a large students' common room, the arena in which pulpit gladiators fought, mixing metaphors and chopping logic. The assembly hall was on the first floor. On the same floor were small classrooms and the famous room at the end of the corridor where trial sermons were preached and many tears shed.

Friday afternoon was the great occasion when the "guv'-nor," as Spurgeon was affectionately described, gave his lecture and afterward joined the men at tea. In later years the tea drinking gave way to interviews with students in the little room at the top of the stairs—a holy of holies, to many men. Spurgeon interviewed applicants for the ministry and talked with students about their difficulties and hopes.

No man could have meant more to his boys than this great leader to his raw recruits. If the walls could speak, what stories they might tell! Spurgeon was a father confessor, very approachable. In his tabernacle room servant girls, persons in high positions, street hawkers, and scholars told the secrets of their hearts. Spurgeon was a true physician of souls. No one went to him in despair and came away without hope.

It was an unforgettable experience to enter that little room for the first time. My own impressions mimic those of hundreds. Spurgeon spoke to me of the ministry as a vocation and asked questions now quite forgotten. He seemed hardly satisfied with the replies. Moving uneasily in his chair, he said, "There are many of our men in the ministry very poor, and not a few are regarded as fools. Why do you want to join their number?"

I had not thought of hardship or reputation.

"No," he said, looking straight into my eyes, "there is less money in it than you may now be earning and no social status."

Then he rose from his chair, leaning heavily on his stick. For a moment his face clouded with physical pain. He sat down again and talked about preaching as if there could be nothing greater on earth or in heaven than to proclaim the gospel.

How wonderfully he could talk in private—as in public—concerning his Lord. There was no doubt about the good news.

"You shall come into college," he finally said to me.

From that moment I was one of "Spurgeon's men," glorying in the nickname even when it was spoken disdainfully. Like others, I did not always agree with my chief but I swore fealty. It was not discipleship but devotion. In that room, many a student rose from his knees with misty eyes. No words would come. But the "guv'nor" understood. There was a light in his eyes—rare in the gaze of a stern man, rather like a mother's expression as she kisses the child she loves.

Among his men, the "guv'nor's" table talk was wiser than most men's philosophy. To know Spurgeon was a liberal education for the ministry. His Friday readings were first-class lessons in elocution. He could make the English Bible live.

One such Friday afternoon in the college hall the "guv'-nor" sat at his desk and talked. Spurgeon had been at Menton. The sixty or seventy students were reinforced by London ministers and distinguished visitors. There was excitement when the door opened and the "guv'nor" entered, leaning heavily on his stick. The men rose and the rafters rang. Spurgeon was pleased as a child with their welcome. He made his way to the platform and sat in the old seat, a striking figure with his massive head covered with gray-tinged hair, shaggy eyebrows, and drooping lids half covering the tired eyes, thick lips, and heavy jaws.

He quietly rose and extended his hand—the indication for prayer. His supplications were tender and sweet. His following address was devotional. Spurgeon's countenance was literally transfigured as he described the increasing preciousness of the "Unseen but not Unknown." The assembly was spellbound. The speaker was absolutely forgotten.

The surroundings of the college were gray. Outside were mean streets. Inside, all was plain as could be—yet no Mecca had ever been more beautiful or sacred as on that afternoon.

Spurgeon was most at home with his boys. Genius never grows up; in many ways the "guv'nor" was just a boy, absolutely confident in himself and others. He was easily imposed upon, and his sympathies readily responded to appeals.

One afternoon he said he had received a serious complaint from the affluent treasurer of a village chapel who was grieved by the mercenary spirit of a student who preached indifferent sermons. The students were all ears. Who was it? And what would the "guv'nor" say to him?

With a merry twinkle, Spurgeon added, "Our brother received ten and sixpence as a fee, and the railway fare amounted to seven and elevenpence."

Turning to his private secretary, he remarked, "Harrald, write and tell him not to have any more sermons of the shilling and three-pence halfpenny sort but to pay for those of a better quality."

Illustrious visitors from all over the world found their way to the college for special conferences. Moody and Sankey during their mission to London were welcomed there. The conferences offered opportunities for old students to compare notes and listen not only to the "guv'nor" but to some of the foremost men in the country. Spurgeon welcomed meetings in his own home. The beautiful grounds in the rear of his garden provided opportunities for social intercourse and for games—cricket, bowls, tennis, and darts—while Spurgeon sat under the tree interviewing men who sought advice.

Spurgeon never seemed to forget a student, even after an absence of years. The "guv'nor" would inquire about the progress of the man's church and the members of his family, often naming them. It was Spurgeon's custom to keep in touch. He wrote personal letters when students settled into a pastorate or considered changing careers. The Reverend T. Hancocks of Ramsgate kept a treasured sheet of faded notepaper. One paragraph of its advice read:

> *Never be satisfied with yourself but go on growing, for we need men fitted to take the better positions, even more than we do the rank and file. Stick to your study even when you are in the midst of ministerial work, for you must be replenished continually or you cannot give out to others.*

At one time he addressed a personal letter to each of the children of his former students. They expressed tender hope for the child's future and a deep desire that each should know the Savior.

Spurgeon's brother, James, vice president of the college, was a friend to all the students. He was ever accessible to those in any kind of difficulty. His brother wisely recognized that "Mr. James" was best able to deal with questions of administration. For years James presided over the tabernacle officers' meetings, and every detail was safe in his care.

James was an incomparable complement to his brother. It was beautiful to watch their happy relationship. Even in later years, when James felt it his duty to remain in the Baptist Union, it did not mean any lack of affection on Spurgeon's part for his brother.

No sketch of the college would be complete without a brief biography of some of its early students. Pastor Frank White, described as "Professor of Buttonhole Theology" for his proficiency at getting hold of people, led to Christ the author Charles Reade. Archibald Brown carried the college banner to East London, gathering a great congregation in the tabernacle on Bow Road; for many years, Brown's congregation was second in size only to Spurgeon's. William Cuff went to Shoreditch and built a new church. W. Williams became minister of Upton Chapel and attracted a considerable congregation almost under the shadow of the tabernacle.

John Wilson, who left his father's farm to enter college, went to an empty chapel in Greenwich, out of which grew the wonderful Woolwich Tabernacle. Thomas Greenwood was of great help to London churches and the Baptist Union. John Bradford's name is forever associated with the London Baptist Association.

The college more than justified its existence. Evangelical in its constitution, it focused on academic attainment, realizing the need for educated ministers. Many of its students went on to become presidents of the Baptist Union. James Clarke, editor of the *Christian World*, obtained one hundred pounds for the institution through his paper and spoke highly of its work. He and Spurgeon maintained a good relationship, although as the years passed their theological differences became more pronounced.

Spurgeon urged his students to find their own voice rather than imitate his. Hence, his students were known for their individuality. Spurgeon loved to hear of their adventures in preaching the gospel in the marketplace or the hired room of a wayside inn, where someone who heard the good news professed allegiance to Christ.

Spurgeon encouraged them to cultivate new ground. He wanted more Baptist churches established in and around London. He would pay the rent of a hired room for six or twelve months. If, at the end of that time, the experiment justified the expenditure, he would go on; if not, the student moved to another "pitch."

TEN

The love stories of preachers might prove an interesting study. Jonathan Edwards was at his best in his love letters, and John Calvin very human in his correspondence. Their letters tell stories that should be remembered.

Spurgeon's love story is quaint and intriguing.

The daily press on January 12, 1856, devoted much attention to the marriage of a popular preacher. One of the journals recorded:

> *On Tuesday morning, an unusual scene was witnessed in the neighborhood of Park Street Chapel, Southwark, a large building, belonging to the Baptist body of dissenters, at the rear of the Borough Market. Of this place of worship, the minister is the Reverend C. H. Spurgeon, a very young man, who, some months since, produced an extraordinary degree of interest at Exeter Hall, where he preached during the time his chapel was in course of enlargement.*

On Tuesday morning the popular young preacher was married. Shortly after eight o'clock, although the morning was dark, damp, and cold, as many as five hundred ladies, in light and gay attire, besieged the doors of the chapel, accompanied by many gentlemen, members of the congregation, and personal friends. From that hour the crowd increased so rapidly that the thoroughfare was blocked up against vehicles and pedestrians, and a body of the "M" Division of Police had to be sent for to prevent accidents. When the chapel doors were opened there was a terrific rush, and in less than half an hour the doors were closed upon many of the eager visitors who, like the earlier and more fortunate comers, were favored with tickets of admission.

The bride was Miss Susannah Thompson, only daughter of Mr. Thompson, of Falcon Square, London, and the ceremony was performed by the Reverend Dr. Alexander Fletcher, of Finsbury Chapel. At the close of the ceremony, the congratulations of the congregation were tendered to the newly married pair with the heartiest goodwill.

Spurgeon's originality was nowhere more conspicuous than in his courtship. Miss Thompson had a wooing that would have surprised any maiden. It began with a present of an illustrated copy of *The Pilgrim's Progress*, with a three-line message expressing sincere desire for her progress in the blessed pilgrimage.

The young couple were accidentally—or providentially? —included in the same party on the opening of the Crystal Palace in June 1854. They sat side by side on raised seats at the end of the auditorium. Amid the buzz of conversation, waiting for the pageant to begin, Spurgeon passed a little book to the girl at his side, pointed to a selected passage, and asked her opinion. The volume was Martin Tupper's *Proverbial Philosophy*. The quotation was on marriage, and began: "Seek a good wife of thy God, for she is the best gift of His Providence."

While she read the lines and a glow came to her cheeks, a voice whispered, "Do you pray for him who is to be your husband?" She was not sure what she replied, or whether she answered at all.

The voice said, "Will you walk round the palace with me?" A nod of the head was her answer.

Their friends "accidentally" left them alone. In August the engagement of Miss Thompson to the Reverend C. H. Spurgeon was made public. She became a regular attender at New Park Street Chapel and was baptized by the pastor.

At the end of 1855, Spurgeon sent his last gift to Miss Thompson: a copy of the first volume of his sermons in *The Pulpit Library*. Until the end, she was his beloved helper in all his work, and he delighted in paying tribute to the angel of his home. He made John Ploughman say, "Matrimony came from Paradise and leads to it. I was never half so happy before I was a married man as I am now."

Their early household was modest. Even when they went to Westwood, they were careful to avoid excessive display. It would not be exaggerating to say that for every pound they spent on themselves they spent five times more in the work of their Master, often curtailing their own pleasures so one of the institutions might be kept from disaster.

At the end of a Sabbath's duties he would sit in an easy chair by the fire while "Susie" read a page or two of Good Master George Herbert. Sometimes the end of the day found him very depressed, and then the ministry of "the pastor's pastor" was a benediction.

Twin sons, Thomas and Charles, brightened their home and gave life new meaning. Spurgeon was a great lover of little children.

The love story between Spurgeon and his wife lost none of its romance with the passing years but rather grew in tender intensity. Mrs. Spurgeon supplemented the work of her husband. She was known among the ministers of all denominations for dispensing gifts of books and later for sending boxes of clothes to the families of village ministers. Her autobiography is a love lyric detailing her home life.

Mrs. Spurgeon was an invalid much of her life. She was a fine example of the triumph of sanctified will over physical suffering. Even in pain, she dictated many letters to other sufferers and helped bear the burdens of ministers of all denominations who had fallen on evil times. The Book Fund was Mrs. Spurgeon's creation, started with money saved from her housekeeping. During her lifetime the fund sent thousands of volumes to the studies of pastors all over the land.

Writing from Menton in early 1891, Spurgeon told a friend of the "Samaritan work" done quietly by his wife. "She has been very ill since you saw her but spending her 'cow money' on her daily eleven gallons of soup and loaves of bread has kept her from fretting."

Spurgeon's favorite cow gave an extra supply of pure milk, part of which Mrs. Spurgeon sold to help the funds of the soup kitchen in which she was particularly interested. Her average profits, with a little added, enabled her all through the winter to provide soup and bread daily for hungry children.

Spurgeon, meanwhile, did his best to help pastors who were compelled to live on a pittance.

Spurgeon's second home on the outskirts of London was Helensburgh House, Nightingale Lane, Clapham. He thought the house would be too expensive to maintain but his wife disagreed. The advantages of the general surroundings, the high ground, better accommodations, and, above all, plenty of space for the children to play settled the matter. The home was actually quite modest.

The preacher was a great lover of the domestic side of life. He often expressed regret that he had a beautiful garden and no time to enjoy it. The home on Nightingale Lane had a neat little garden in front and delightful grounds in the rear. It was here that Spurgeon satisfied one of his ambitions: He kept a cow. He was very proud of his cow and could tell almost to the pint the average milk the cow gave.

Spurgeon sometimes managed to get away with his wife for a walk in the country lanes around their home. Mrs. Spurgeon loved flowers, and they would find many wildflowers on their journeys. Spurgeon especially loved ferns. His fernery at Nightingale Lane and afterward at Westwood was a special feature he proudly showed to his privileged guests; sometimes as a mark of affection he gave a little fern to be taken away. American visitors took pride in carrying them across the Atlantic, displaying them and telling of a walk with Spurgeon around his garden.

It was at Helensburgh House that John Ruskin frequently visited Spurgeon. He gave a hundred pounds to the tabernacle project, and their many letters breathed affection. Once he was deeply moved to find Spurgeon sick. He begged him to take life less strenuously.

Spurgeon's library contained almost all Ruskin's works inscribed by the author. One day Ruskin told him a remarkable story. A widower with several children was visiting an old farmhouse he considered buying. While he talked with the agent, the children were allowed to inspect the place. After exhausting the wonders above ground, they discovered a basement and headed downstairs. Midway, they were frightened. Standing at the bottom of the stairs they saw their mother, with outstretched arms and a loving gesture, waving them back. With cries of fear and joy they turned and ran to their father. "Mother has come back!" they said.

When a search was made, it was discovered that at the bottom of the stairs was a deep, open well, entirely unguarded. Had the children continued running down into the darkness, they undoubtedly would have fallen into the well and drowned.

In the little garden on Nightingale Lane, Spurgeon began the practice of receiving college students, which he continued for many years. In the early days, when the students were few, they went regularly on Saturday mornings for informal talks with the president. Later, when the school of prophets numbered a hundred and the meetings were at Westwood, they went on special occasions. The president opened his home and heart generously to all the brethren.

Ultimately the Spurgeons had to move. Nightingale Lane had lost its rural character. Houses had sprung up, and the traffic made it impossible for Spurgeon to take his walks without attracting much attention.

Their move to Westwood, Beulah Hill, bore a touch of romance. One of the neighbors on Nightingale Lane wanted a house for his son-in-law and casually inquired whether Spurgeon would like to sell. A day or two before, Spurgeon had seen a board announcing the Westwood premises for sale. It was found that the price of Helensburgh House was about the same as that of Westwood. Spurgeon always thought Westwood "a little too grand for me," but he loved it nevertheless and took great joy moving into his new home.

Spurgeon's door was always open. No doubt his hospitality was frequently abused. Missionaries, preachers, and public men from all over the world found their way to Westwood. Spurgeon was a courteous and generous host who loved to entertain, and he was a great talker.

Spurgeon took broad views of things that often surprised his friends, and he astonished them with the extent of his knowledge of obscure subjects. With unfeigned delight he would accompany his visitors through the gardens, indicating rare flowers and ferns that had been given to him. In the library he would point out first editions of rare books. He once remarked, "My Master, I am sure, does not grudge me the enjoyment of my garden. I owe it to Him. I love it and praise Him for it."

Those privileged to sit in his study caught something of the spirit of the worker. The room was large and beautifully but not elaborately furnished. It was, as he described it, a place for work. His two secretaries, Mr. Harrald and J. L. Keys, sat on opposite sides of the room. Sometimes one or two others would be at the long table, proofreading or handling correspondence. Harrald normally had the routine correspondence, Keys the literary work but often there was too much for them to do alone, and friends were called in to help.

Spurgeon would sit at the end of the room with his back to the little private sanctum to which he often retired for prayer. He had an amazing capacity for work. He would dictate by the hour, go to his little room, and return in a few moments to begin again.

The "Question" oak was so named because beneath its shade Spurgeon would sit with the students on the grass before him, while they kept up a running stream of questions about their work, their study, and almost anything of human interest. The answers were given almost as soon as the questions were asked. Spurgeon's knowledge of biblical subjects was extensive. Often he would suggest an alternative translation of the old text and would refer to illustrations in forgotten volumes. His answers were enlivened with humor and puns. Wit and wisdom were so blended that an unforgettable impression was made on the minds of those present.

Spurgeon greatly loved animals. At one time Westwood was home to three pugs: Punch and Judy and little Gyp. When Spurgeon was in southern France, his letters home would ask for news about the dogs.

I shall never forget my introduction to Punch and Judy. They were in the room where the "guv'nor" had been telling me of some work he wanted done. He said casually, "We will pray about it."

At that moment one of the pugs began to walk across the carpet. "Punch and Judy, come here," he said. "Master is going to pray."

Punch and Judy came close to his feet and settled down with bowed heads. I was too amused to do anything but smile broadly. When Spurgeon opened his eyes he said, "Yes, they are funny. The Lord must love humor or He never would have made their faces."

The horses that took Spurgeon to the tabernacle were very dear to him. He talked with them as though they were children. He also loved birds; he had a little sanctuary from which he drew not only pleasure but many illustrations.

A mere record of the names of visitors to Westwood would almost provide an index of the famous people of Spurgeon's time. Among those who shared his hospitality were several bishops. The letters Mrs. Spurgeon received during her husband's last illness and after his homegoing indicate a genuine friendship between unlikely people.

Spurgeon was very interested in handwriting. His own penmanship was almost copperplate. He believed a great deal about a person's character was indicated by the way he or she wrote. He obtained a fine collection of autographs and would talk excitedly of the signatures of Lincoln and Oliver Cromwell.

He also was fascinated by architecture. Among his earliest hobbies was collecting prints of cathedrals of many lands. He would discuss the curves and lines of each building and the superiority of Grecian over Gothic design. When the architect of the Pastors' College buildings explained his plans to Spurgeon, he was surprised to discover how much Spurgeon knew about construction and architecture.

In the early days he had shown a gift for sketching. His sons were both at home with pencil and brush. Young Charles painted good portraits, particularly of his father, while Thomas was accomplished enough in watercolors to hold a successful one-man exhibition.

When the boys left home, they went to boarding school and finally found their way to the Pastors' College. Charles held pastorates at Greenwich, Nottingham, and Cheltenham. He was an above-average preacher and a genial personality. He found his lifework as governor of the Stockwell Orphanage, where he was loved as the wise father of a very large family.

Thomas's work is well-known. It is not too much to say both sons possessed gifts that would have been more highly valued had they not been continuously compared with their father.

ELEVEN

When C. H. Spurgeon entered the pulpit in New Park Street, a prince of preachers came to his throne. There were men who mumbled and fumbled in their speech, and others who delivered Johnsonian sentences without Johnsonian wisdom. A few brilliant men were preaching a beautiful humanism, tinged with theism but their efforts were limited. The Church of England's popular men were mainly of the High Calvinist school, and they were hard to find.

Spurgeon introduced a new element into preaching. His lectures on preaching are among the best. His ideal was that of the fisherman. He lowered his net to catch fish; he baited his hook, not for decorative purposes but to secure souls.

"Sermons," Spurgeon wrote, "should have real teaching in them, and their doctrine should be solid, substantial, and abundant. We do not enter the pulpit to talk for talk's sake." He insisted the preacher must proclaim Christ always and everywhere. Christ's Person, offices, and work must be "our one great all-comprehending theme. The world still needs to be told of its Savior and of the way to reach Him."

Spurgeon insisted from the first that nothing could compensate for the absence of teaching. He insisted on practicality. Some think in smoke and preach in clouds; Spurgeon was concerned that the people understand his meaning. Clear expression is not a natural gift; it comes with practice, and the prince of preachers was continually clarifying his thought.

He admonished his students that no matter what their genius might be, nothing would make up for the absence of personal study. Fluent speech and impromptu wit were to be regarded as dangerous. "If you seek these gifts as pillows for an idle head, you will be much mistaken, for the possession of this noble power will involve you in a vast amount of labor in order to increase and retain it."

He constantly cultivated the homiletic habit. He told his students:

> *Occasionally one has heard or read of men agreeing by way of bravado to preach upon texts given them at the time in the pulpit or in the vestry. Such vainglorious displays are disgusting and border on profanity. As well might we have exhibitions of juggling on the Sabbath as such mountebankery of oratory.*

Dr. O. S. Davis, president of Chicago Theological Seminary, analyzed one of Spurgeon's most famous sermons, "Songs in the Night." It had been said the sermon was preached almost on the spur of the moment. But Davis pointed to the number of illustrations, quotations, and figures of speech. It was an amazing production. Davis said:

The sermon could not possibly be confused with an essay or oration. The note of certainty is constantly sounded. The preacher is sure that he has something to give which will produce songs in the night. The divisions are clearly indicated and show the lines of thought to be followed.

Davis called attention to the biblical character of the sermon and the appeal at the end. It was Spurgeon's business to bear testimony and press for a verdict.

Spurgeon's style resulted from almost a lifetime of practice. In the early days at Waterbeach, he wrote his sermons fully. In later years he wrote two or three pages and then began the practice of dictating. His secretaries were constantly on the lookout for illustrations for their chief. J. L. Keys spent hours each week in research at the British Museum.

Dictating to a secretary enabled Spurgeon to speak with precision. He gave great attention to the choice of words and familiarized himself with Saxon terms. His style was homely—not cheap or vulgar but within the mental range of the average audience. He did not preach for the elite, though many from the intelligentsia sat at his feet and regarded him as a great stylist.

There was nothing haphazard about his work. In a lecture on the choice of text, he said:

I frequently sit hour after hour praying and waiting for a subject, and this is the main part of my study; much hard labor have I spent in manipulating topics, ruminating upon points of doctrine, making skeletons out of verses and then burying every bone of them in the catacombs of oblivion, sailing on and on over leagues of broken water till I see the red lights and make sail direct to the desired haven.

Unstudied thoughts coming from the mind without previous research, without the subjects in hand having been investigated at all, must be of a very inferior quality, even from the most superior men, and as none of us would have the effrontery to glorify ourselves as men of genius or wonders of erudition, I fear that our unpremeditated thoughts upon most subjects would not be remarkably worthy of attention.

Our sermons should be our mental lifeblood— the outflow of our intellectual and spiritual vigor; or, to change the figure, they should be diamonds well cut and well set, precious intrinsically and bearing the marks of labor. God forbid that we should offer to the Lord that which costs us nothing.

Spurgeon paid great attention to his sermons' opening passages. He valued the first sentences as setting out what he proposed to do, indicating the road along which he would lead the thought of the congregation. His opening usually placed his hearers in the very center of the subject. Unnecessary words were eliminated.

The greatest artists have always been more concerned with life than with art. Art is a means to an end, and Spurgeon used his marvelous gift for a definite purpose. It was easy to listen to his words without being conscious of the art with which they were spoken. He would not wear anything that attracted attention, and every moment was so exquisitely perfect that it gave the intended emphasis almost without being observed.

I often have wished I could have drawn a portrait of

Spurgeon as I sometimes saw him in the old days, on the Sunday mornings when the tabernacle was packed from end to end. He would come down the little flight of stairs from the room where he had been alone with God to the platform where he would be before the eager gaze of five to six thousand people. For more than thirty years the great congregations came twice every Sunday and were not disappointed.

The first time I saw him, the building was strange to me. The congregation was overwhelming—such a mixed crowd, with the well groomed and the ill clad side by side. There was a strange expectancy in their eyes and a hush almost awe-inspiring as the lonely figure hobbled down the stairs. He was of medium height but seemed shorter because of his girth. He was dressed as an ordinary country gentleman, with nothing clerical to indicate his profession.

He grasped the side of a pew as he passed down, leaning on a stick, evidently moving with difficulty. He reached the front of the platform with hand uplifted. In a voice clear as the notes of a flute, he said, "Let us pray." There was scarcely the sound of a breath while the strong, country-bred man talked to our Father with almost childlike simplicity and tenderness.

After the prayer a tall, thin man came to the front, tuning fork in hand. He pitched the tune and led the hymn. The voices of thousands of people sang with gladness, like the movement of vast waters. There was no need of an organ.

The reading of the scriptures, with brief interjections, seemed strange but enlightening. A special feature of Sunday services was Spurgeon's comments—almost lectures—on the scripture reading; it is a calamity they were not reported. This was followed by the sermon.

The preacher had been sitting in his chair, moving as though nervous or in pain, while a number of announcements of weekly engagements were made. He straightened himself with difficulty and stood at full height. The voice announcing the text was low and pleasant and could be heard all over the building. As the preacher proceeded, his pain was forgotten. The countenance, heavy and uninteresting, was changed. The dull, sleepy eyes lit up until they glowed. The theme took possession of the speaker. He ceased to be conscious of himself. He had become a voice.

His was probably the most wonderful voice God ever made. His imagination had the quality of the poet, and he spoke with the earnest sincerity of the flaming evangelist. To him, every occasion was a crisis. He believed human destiny might be determined there and then. Tremendous faith colored all his preaching.

For nearly an hour he made all those people forget their drab surroundings and commonplace lives. They smiled broadly at a humorous aside and wiped their eyes at a moving passage.

After the sermon, as the last hymn was announced, one became conscious once more of the surroundings, which had been obliterated by the magic of the preacher's oratory.

During one of his lectures, Spurgeon told his students it should be possible for a speaker to whisper and have the words heard over a large building. They looked incredulous.

"You do not think so? Very well, gentlemen, adjourn to the tabernacle and scatter over the building."

The students trooped across the college yard to the great tabernacle and scattered to the back of the top gallery and the end seats. Spurgeon came to the pulpit with a smile. Holding up his hand, he whispered, "Gentlemen, if you hear what I say, show your pocket handkerchiefs."

From all over the building, pocket handkerchiefs were exhibited by more than sixty men. Then in trumpet tones he called, "Gentlemen, put them away. They are not quite clean."

The ministry at the tabernacle was far too heavy for one man. The Reverend J. A. Spurgeon was invited to relieve his brother of part of the responsibility, and for many years the partnership was happy and unbroken. Crowds continued to throng to the regular services. Not content to preach twice on Sunday and once during the week, Spurgeon went from church to church, preaching on special occasions and helping the great societies in their annual gatherings.

During 1863, 311 people were baptized in the tabernacle, while 116 were received by letters of commendation. After deductions, the total number of members stood at 2,517. Year by year the numbers grew until the tabernacle had the largest membership of any English-speaking church in the world.

Eventually, a vacation in London was regarded as incomplete unless it included visits to St. Paul's and Spurgeon's tabernacle. People of all ranks found their way to the tabernacle. It was rumored that Her Majesty, Queen Victoria, had attended a service. There was no doubt the prime minister, Gladstone, did so in 1882. The Grand Old Man and his son joined the pastor in his private room.

But Spurgeon did not go out of his way to court the favor of the high and mighty. In the early years of the tabernacle ministry, Spurgeon devoted special attention to pastoral work. It is amazing he could find time to become known to his church families. In some circles he was particularly at home. William Olney and his family were almost as intimate as relatives. The Greenwoods' doors were always open to give sanctuary to the tired preacher.

When cholera swept the district, Spurgeon devoted himself unreservedly to visiting the sick and dying. One dismal afternoon, exhausted, he passed a shop window on the Dover Road and read the text: "There shall no evil befall thee, neither shall any plague come nigh thy dwelling."

Spurgeon devoted much time and thought to public and private prayer. He astonished a company of ministers by advising them to prepare their prayers—not the wording but the topics—and, most of all, to prepare themselves to pray. Prayer is the avenue by which the conscious life of God is entered. It is not simply waiting on the Lord, making confession or giving praise; to Spurgeon it was abandoning oneself to the consciousness of the Presence.

What student ever forgot the final interview in the "guv'nor's" rooms just before leaving college, which invariably was terminated with a brief prayer dedicating the man to his lifework. The heavens seemed to open and the Spirit descend.

Spurgeon lived a disciplined life. The amount of work he accomplished was amazing. He would dictate to three secretaries in succession and then turn to the study of a fresh subject as though he were just beginning his work for the day. He read enormously: biographies, histories, and the classics. Few possessed anything like his acquaintance with the Puritan fathers. Shakespeare's plays and Milton's poems pleased him. In fiction, Sir Walter Scott and Charles Dickens were his favorites; he found the immortal "Sam Weller" hilarious.

London pulpits in Spurgeon's time had a number of preachers of outstanding reputation. Joseph Parker was at the City Temple, Guinness Rogers at Clapham, John Clifford at Praed Street, William Brock at Bloomsbury, Henry Allon at Islington, Newman Hall at Lambeth, Canon Liddon at St.

Paul's, and Dean Stanley at the Abbey, with Canon Farrar towering above them all. But alone, like an Alpine peak, was Spurgeon, with a glory all his own.

Sermons naturally fall under one of three headings, structurally. There are those which are written in full and read, those which are written in full and delivered either from headings or without notes, and those which are preached extemporaneously or from brief notes. Spurgeon, unlike many great preachers, did not write much. He was accustomed to dictating and then revising the sermon. It would be impossible to say how much time he gave to the preparation of any one sermon.

Ward Beecher was said to have described his own method thus:

I am like a man who has an apple tree in his garden and knows that some of the apples are ripe. He reaches up and feels expectantly among the many hanging on the boughs, till at last one drops readily into his hand and he crunches it with joy. So, when I am getting ready for Sunday morning, I feel through my mind to find a thought that has been slowly ripening through experience. It falls naturally toward me, and I bite into it with relish.

Dr. Fosdick described his method:

For myself I can only say that I always have my theme for the following Sunday chosen by Tuesday morning, and I work steadfastly Tuesday, Wednesday, Thursday, Friday, and Saturday mornings on the development of the theme but I always write in order to clarify and define my thoughts, then I draw

off an outline of what I have written and speak
from the outline I have made.

Dr. Parkes Cadman, an American radio preacher, told of his method:

In making a sermon I first of all fix my mind on a
suitable theme and then try to find a text that fits it.
Sometimes the process is reversed and a great verse
from scripture leaps into my mind like a tiger from a
thicket. I then assemble all the literature I can muster
which has bearing upon the matter and con it over. I
afterwards write out the sermon in my own hand.

All men of genius give the impression they are working with ease and almost without effort. To the unknowing, it seemed easy for Spurgeon to stand up in the tabernacle and preach. People remarked as they left the building, "I have often felt what he said." He was a true doctor of souls—not a general practitioner but a specialist in the holy art of representing Christ to the people. He loved his people and gave every last ounce of himself for them.

After twenty-five years, a public testimonial was presented to the pastor. More than six thousand pounds was collected and given to him May 20, 1879. William Olney testified:

The generosity of our pastor, his self-abnegation and
his self-denial should be clearly understood. . . .
When he first came at the invitation of the church
we were a few feeble folk; the sittings at Park Street
had for some years gone a-begging; the minister's
salary was exceedingly small; and the difficulty we

had in keeping the doors open was very great. Incidental and other expenses of one sort and another were a heavy burden upon the people. When Mr. Spurgeon came the old arrangement was continued: Whatever the seat rents produced should be his. In former years the amount was supplemented by a number of collections; when Mr. Spurgeon came everything was changed. The seats were occupied and the money belonged to him. At the close of three months he said, "We will have no more collections for incidental expenses. I shall pay for the cleaning and lighting and what is required myself." And from that time until now he has done so.

Olney concluded:

Mr. Spurgeon is a great example of giving. When he was pressed to receive this testimonial he declared that he would accept it on one condition: "Not one farthing for myself. You may give it to me for myself if you like but I will not keep it; it shall all be the Lord's." And it was.

In 1884, when Mr. Spurgeon's jubilee was celebrated, another testimonial was presented to him. The sum was 4,500 pounds, and again he insisted on devoting it all to the Lord's work. His private generosity was known throughout the land. He usually would send a five-pound note, but what was more welcome was the little letter: "Dear friend, please use this for me but be sure to use it upon yourself and your loved ones. Yours as ever, C. H. S."

TWELVE

In the generally accepted meaning of the phrase, Spurgeon was not a social reformer; that is, he did not spend his time advocating schemes for social betterment. He took little part in parliamentary elections, though for many years he was a keen Liberal with leanings to the Radical wing. He followed Gladstone until the tension over home rule, then went with John Bright and Joseph Chamberlain.

Spurgeon was interested in many forms of social work. The mere fact that his church supported a large number of missions in slum areas and engaged heavily in social service showed his sympathies. One of his last acts was an encouraging communication to his friend, John Groom. Groom had conceived the idea of teaching physically disabled girls to make artificial flowers. Spurgeon was deeply interested and approved the suggestion. The enterprise grew into a great organization.

Spurgeon also stood by Charles Montague, who began a labor of love among the poor of Spitalfields. Montague secured an unused cowshed, had it whitewashed and disinfected, and opened it as a Sunday school and mission hall on Sundays, and a clubhouse during the week. The work grew for the advancement of young people.

The story of the Stockwell Orphanage often has been told. In an 1884 sermon, Spurgeon said:

> *It is striking to see, as you and I did see, a woman of moderate wealth discarding all the comforts of life in order to save sufficient funds to start an orphanage in which the children might be cared for, not merely, as she said, for the children's sake but for Christ's sake, that He might be glorified.*

Spurgeon was asked by the orphan's benefactor, Mrs. Hillyard, to administer the funds for founding the facility. Both Thomas Spurgeon and his brother, Charles, ultimately served as presidents of the orphanage. The nondenominational institution brought music and sunshine into the lives of thousands of children, some of whom gave their lives to the Lord's service as missionaries and ministers. Spurgeon's appearance among the children was hailed with delight. Successive generations of little people sat at his knees in open-eyed wonder while he told them marvelous stories and examined the progress they made.

One of Spurgeon's last public appearances was at the Metropolitan Music Hall on Edgware Road, on behalf of the Hyde Park Open-Air Mission. He was very interested in the work of Charles Cook, who spent a great deal of money and time working among prison inmates in England and abroad. Cook secured many reforms and always found a sympathetic supporter in Spurgeon.

Elderly poor people had a very hard time in Spurgeon's

day. His tabernacle arranged for the provision of new schools for the young and almshouses for the elderly with proceeds from a property sale. For years, Spurgeon paid the utility expenses from his own pocket; few people knew he was the largest contributor to the effort.

William Orsman was a civil servant who devoted his life to the down-and-out in the courts and alleys of Hoxton. He provided shelter for the homeless before the Salvation Army or the Church Army began their work. Orsman was greatly supported and inspired by Spurgeon.

All the tabernacle missions were centers of social influence. Spurgeon believed in keeping to his own work of preaching the gospel but he was not indifferent to the weekday life of the people.

He was concerned with providing wholesome reading. In 1866 he called together a few young men to whom he unfolded a dream. He thought they might become peddlers of good books, going from house to house—not simply selling wholesome literature that would counteract wicked popular materials but having the opportunity to be comrades to the sick and infirm. He suggested the foundation of a literary brotherhood.

The dream came true with the formation of the Colportage Society. Though it was difficult to see where the money would come from to support it, six men were employed. By 1874 the work had grown, and thirty-five men were employed. Later the number increased to fifty, with annual sales totaling more than three thousand pounds.

Many amusing schemes for social betterment were brought to Spurgeon's notice. He feared ministers being sidetracked into work for which they had no aptitude—work which, it seemed to him, could be done better by laymen. His policy was to excite others to go forth, fulfilling the necessary tasks and fighting the battles of the oppressed.

During the time of the series of strikes culminating in the great dock strike, he gave his support quietly but definitely to those who were struggling for the very means of existence. On one occasion there was a strike at a tannery; about forty men came out because of a cut in wages. The tannery belonged to Samuel Barrow & Brother. The senior partner was closely associated with the tabernacle, and the brother, who afterward became Sir Reuben Barrow, was an officer at West Croydon Church, where Dr. Spurgeon was pastor.

Spurgeon was very concerned. He knew the senior partner was greatly troubled and feared some of the men and their families were short of food. The next day Samuel Barrow sent for me, and unknown to the men on strike, he provided subscriptions to a relief fund that enabled the men to continue their opposition until a settlement was agreed upon. Spurgeon and Barrow both greatly enjoyed the joke.

Social service may be divided into two parts: talking and doing. There are those who become eloquent about the condition of slum dwellers and old people. There are the others who serve; they may have little gift of speech but they do the work. Spurgeon believed in doing what he could to change conditions by changing individuals. His theory was that the changed life transforms the circumstances.

What is now familiarly known as social service, was, from Spurgeon's point of view, the ordinary expression of Christian character. He firmly believed the best description of pure religion was that given by the apostle James: "Pure religion and undefiled before God and the Father is this, To visit the fatherless and widows in their affliction, and to keep himself unspotted from the world."

THIRTEEN

From the earliest years, Spurgeon was drawn to journalism. From the time when, as a child, he planned his own magazine and wrote most of the contents to the last hours, he felt the attractions of the press.

An interesting souvenir came into my hands. It is a tiny, sixteen-page, handwritten magazine, measuring four inches by two and one quarter. It was preserved by a young lady who was governess to the older children of Reverend John Spurgeon's family while he resided at Colchester.

The little publication is one of the curiosities of literature. Spurgeon was under twelve when he produced it—the first of more than a hundred works from his pen. Those who smiled at the boy's ingenuity little guessed his printed volumes would be best-sellers.

The first page reads: "Home Juvenile Society. Vol. 1, April, 1846. Colchester, C. Spurgeon." The second page records: "The editor would be very grateful if someone would write a letter for this magazine. All acknowledgments and notices may be made in this magazine." Page three bears the date, Sunday the twelfth, with: "The prayer meeting this morning was omitted as Mr. Jennings was out, and thus an end was put to it. I hope it will be resumed or else I shall keep to my engagements."

Page four has an announcement: "On Monday April 13 an exhibition was held in order to defray the expenses of the tea party. One member in particular seemed very much pleased."

Page five: "In the evening a tea meeting was held and all the members seemed very much gratified. Louisa was admitted as a member to which all agreed."

Sunday the nineteenth is noted: "Prayer meeting very good. Carry it on and let me say that on [the] twenty-sixth there is another. Blessings come through prayer."

Alas, for the twenty-sixth: "No prayer meeting. What a decline. Imitate the page before. Certainly this morning there is an excuse but only one in the month is dreadful."

The remaining pages are in a lighter vein. Page nine is an attempt at humor: "A gentleman having asked a boy how old he was, replied, 'Eight, sir.' 'How old is your brother?' 'Seven, sir, but when one more year has passed we shall be both of the same age.'"

Page ten philosophizes: "There is every prospect of success to our society, for other societies have succeeded, then why should not ours? It is true there is a difference in number of members, amount of money, age—these are all compensated for by our unity, ready hearts and growth.

"Then do not despair. Every hope belonging to others, belongs to us."

There are two quotations on greatness. The first: "One of the later kings of Spain, unsuccessful in war, had lost various considerable provinces. His flatterers gave him the title of 'Great.' 'His greatness,' remarked a Spaniard, 'resembles the extent of ditches which increases according to the quantity of ground which is taken away from him.' "

The second: "Leonidas, the leader of the Lacedemonians, was told, when he was about to engage with the Persians, that their arrows obscured the sun by their multitude. He replied, 'Then we shall fight better in the shade.' "

There are two riddles without answers and a concluding paragraph that a new club would be formed to raise tenpence. The little production reveals more of the boy than many of the stories told of his childhood.

During his ministry, one of Spurgeon's first efforts was a column in the *Christian Cabinet*. The little journal represented the theology of the ultra-Calvinists and was too restricted to retain Spurgeon on its staff.

With the Baptist magazine, he worked as joint editor but again there was the difficulty of double harness. He withdrew and announced that he hoped to begin a cheaper magazine. The *Sword and Trowel* was begun in 1865 and from the first was a great success. Individuality is the only way for a newspaper or magazine to succeed. Spurgeon's publication was really Spurgeon.

The announcement of a sermon to be published each week was greeted with ridicule. Amazingly, the circulation of the sermon surpassed all expectations. The publishers had expected to sell five hundred to six hundred copies but from the first it was hardly less than ten times that number. Several sermons reached a circulation of more than a quarter million.

When the five-hundredth sermon was published, a congratulatory meeting was held in the tabernacle. The publishers gave a dinner. Dr. Campbell declared:

*All Mr. Spurgeon's movements have been new. . . . The
idea of preaching and printing a weekly sermon had
never entered the head of anybody but then next to that
in novelty and wonder is the assembly to celebrate the
five-hundredth sermon. Why, Steele with his* Tatlers,
Addison with his Spectators *and Johnson with his*
Ramblers *and* Idlers *were all little men compared
with this stripling. The sale of their papers was limited
to London, while Charles H. Spurgeon has supporters
throughout these isles and all over the world.*

During his first pastorate Spurgeon published the first
of the *Waterbeach Tracts* and contributed a little sketch to
the *Baptist Reporter*. It was his custom to spend Monday
morning revising his copy for the press. He was an exceedingly careful proofreader and a rather severe critic of
any of his helpers who overlooked "little commas." He
must have spent hundreds of hours a year over his correc-
tions, sometimes recasting whole pages.

One of the early volumes, *The Saint and His Savior*, was
sold to the publisher J. S. Virtue for fifty pounds. Spurgeon
thought the amount almost too large for the work but in
comparison to what the book brought to the publisher, it
was a ridiculously small sum. Thirty years later, the copy-
right was offered to Spurgeon, but he declined to pay three
figures for it, reasoning it was cheaper to write another book
than buy that one. One of the largest publishing staffs in
London grew from the business generated by Spurgeon's
material.

The most popular of all Spurgeon's writings were the
little volumes titled *John Ploughman's Talk*. More than three
hundred thousand copies of the first issue were sold in a
short time.

The revenue from his publications would have made Spurgeon a wealthy man but for his great generosity. He had pleaded that the almshouses near the tabernacle be properly endowed but the money was not there in hard times. One morning the trustees received word that five thousand pounds had been given for the endowment. It was not difficult to trace the check to Spurgeon. Early in his career, he believed he would earn a large income by writing and give it to the work of his Master.

Spurgeon contributed literary extracts for Sunday reading to the *Freeman*, the denominational paper. He strove to obtain the cream of religious literature, particularly from little-known authors. The quotations were confined mainly to the Puritans—Wesley and Whitefield, Thomas Hooper, Ambrose and James Durham, and many less well-known writers—and the English classics, including Ruskin's *Modern Painters and Stones of Venice*. The list reflects Spurgeon's reading.

His own published output was greater than that of any other man of his time. It amazed those who knew him. How could he have worked so many years, frequently eighteen hours a day? No preacher of any age or land left his impression on so many lives or was used so largely as a life changer. Single sermons brought hundreds of people to faith in Christ and allegiance to His church.

A poor woman employed by the publishers stole a copy of one of his sermons in which she noticed something she thought she would like to read. She hid the sermon in her bosom and read it at home. The next morning she returned it to the foreman and confessed with tears her theft and her faith in Jesus Christ. The man was so impressed that he, too, was led to a new allegiance. Both found their way to the tabernacle.

An Irish girl in Cork picked up an illustrated cover of one of the sermons and took it home. She read the printing inside and rejoiced to discover the great High Priest who really does absolve us from sin.

A leading London merchant sat with his wife in the lounge of a Riviera hotel. The evening was wet and there was nothing to do. Nobody would take a hand at cards. On the table was a sermon. As a joke, to kill time, he read it and passed it to his wife. They returned to London earlier than they had intended and went to the tabernacle. Both became earnest church workers and intimate friends of the pastor.

Robert Louis Stevenson in *Memories and Portraits* wrote:

> *It was, above all, strange to see Earraid on Sunday, when the sound of the tools ceased and there fell a crystal quiet. All about the green compound, men would be sauntering in their Sunday's best. . . . And it was strange to see our Sabbath services held, as they were, in one of our bothies, with Mr. Brebner reading at a table and the congregation perched about in the double tier of sleeping bunks; and to hear the singing of the psalms, "the chapters," the inevitable Spurgeon's sermon, and the old, eloquent lighthouse prayer.*

The sermons were read on lonely ranches and in mining camps. It was the workers' only bit of Sunday and was very welcome. Men told of long evenings at sea with nothing to read but one or two of Spurgeon's sermons.

The sermon was the center of worship at the tabernacle. The vast congregations really worshiped as they listened to the unfolding of the story that transformed the world. Dr. Richard Glover, a keen and sincere critic, said of Spurgeon,

"In head, in heart, in energy, in spirit, he presented a combination most marvelous and striking. His intellectual qualities, for instance, were of the supreme kind."

Sermons are messages, usually forgotten soon after they are delivered. Sermonic literature is a graveyard of many reputations—yet Spurgeon's sermons survived.

A sermon was published each week for more than sixty-two years, the last appearing May 10, 1917 (No. 3,563). Many of the sermons were translated into other languages.

Spurgeon's controversial writings are the poorest of his works. He was not a controversialist. The sermon on "Baptismal Regeneration" was a powerful composition but owed its enormous circulation to the subject rather than the presentation.

From first to last, Spurgeon was an evangelist, one whose function is to proclaim the Truth. He knew nothing of the art of trimming and compromising. He said what was in his heart and said it clearly. He left no way of escape but burned his bridges every time.

In the early days it was circulated that he taught that children dying in infancy who were not among the elect would be lost. He answered this in a vigorous letter to the *Baptist*:

> *I have never, at any time in my life, said, believed, or imagined that any infant under any circumstances would be cast into hell. I have always believed in the salvation of all infants, and I intensely detest the opinions attributed to me. I do not believe that on this earth there is a professing Christian holding the damnation of infants, or, if there be, he must be insane or utterly ignorant of Christianity.*

Spurgeon's humor sometimes had a rugged if not a rough flavor. But it was perfectly natural and no more offensive or vulgar than the pages of *Punch* in which he delighted. He did not go out of his way to tell funny stories; they came as a matter of course. Some of them were intensely funny. He knew the value of wholesome nonsense and enjoyed it. But he was severe to those whose stories left an unwholesome memory.

John Ploughman's *Talk* was regarded by some literary critics as a great classic of the common people. There was no doubt about its exquisite craftsmanship. There was no suggestion of art and scarcely a word that was not within the limited vocabulary of the ordinary person of the mid-Victorian period. The topics were always timely.

Of religious grumblers, he wrote:

> *He who knows nothing is confident about every-thing. Every clock and even the sundial must be set according to their watches, and the slightest difference from their opinion proves a man to be rotten at heart. Venture to argue with them and their little pot boils over in quick style; ask them for a reason and you might as well go to a sandpit for sugar. They have bottled up the sea of truth and carry it in their waistcoat pockets. They have measured heaven's line of grace and have tied a knot in the string at the exact length of electing love; and as for the things which angels long to know, they have seen them all as boys see sights in a puppet show at the fair.*

The little paper concludes:

Fault-finding is dreadfully catching. One dog will set a whole kennel howling, and the wisest course is to keep out of the way of a man who has the complaint called "the grumbles." The worst of it is that foot-and-mouth disease go together. Good-bye, ye sons of grizzle. John Ploughman would sooner pick a bone in peace than fight for an ox roasted whole.

Spurgeon could be very wise in his nonsense, and he always wrote with a purpose. A paragraph on keeping one's eyes open:

Nobody is more like an honest man than a thorough rogue. When you see a man with a great deal of religion displayed in his shop window, you may depend upon it he keeps a very small stock of it within.

Of things not worth trying:

Don't put a cat on a coach-box or men in places for which they are not fitted. There is no making apples of plums. Little minds will still be little even if you make them beadles or churchwardens. It is a pity to turn a monkey into a minister. Many preachers are good tailors spoilt, and capital shoemakers turned out of their proper calling. When God means a creature to fly He gives it wings, and when He intends men to preach He gives them abilities.

Of great talkers:

I had rather plough all day and be on the road with the wagon all night when it freezes your eyelashes off

*than listen to those great talkers. I had sooner go
without eating till I was as lean as wash-leather than
eat the best turkey that ever came on the table and be
dinned all the while with their awful jaw. They talk
on such a mighty big scale and magnify everything so
thunderingly that you can't believe them when they
accidentally slip in a word or two of the truth. You are
apt to think that even their cheese is chalk.*

The *Salt-Cellars*, a collection of proverbs in two volumes, revealed Spurgeon in a new light. These volumes of
three hundred to four hundred pages each represented an
enormous amount of research and almost incredible reading.
They sold very well. They were drawn from many sources;
not a few sayings were coined by Spurgeon himself, while
hundreds were old ones touched up and many translated
from French or Latin. All his life he kept notebooks to jot
down the gems he discovered in ordinary reading. It was a
joy to him to find an old volume of witty sayings or local
proverbs. He collected calendars and "Garlands of Thought,"
finding amusement and recreation at the end of a long day's
work reading over his stories, arranging them, touching
them up, and putting them into fresh forms, carefully elim-
inating any proverb having an unwholesome suggestion. His
aim was not simply to collect but to select. He regarded
proverbs as the best form of illustration.

He frequently would enliven a drive along a monoto-
nous road with pithy sayings and would express great pleasure if he heard in return a saying that was new to him. He
loved to add to the proverb a bit of his own. For example:
"One swallow does not make a summer. . .but one grasshopper makes many springs." "A drop of gin is a drop too
much. . .why not drop it?"

To some of the proverbs he added illustrations drawn largely from the classics. To "Don't fight over a cheese mite" he added: "It is a pity to contend over a great matter but to quarrel over a mere trifle is never justifiable."

"He preaches well who lives well. . . . Even if he doesn't open his mouth, his example is a sermon."

"Strike while the iron's hot. . .but don't keep on striking till it's cold. Don't preach the people into a good state of mind and then preach them out of it."

Spurgeon's *Salt-Cellars* lasted long after more serious works were forgotten.

FOURTEEN

What Bishop Gore described as "great shocks to established religious belief" came very quietly, almost as silently as the shadows gathering at eventide. Critical science was changing the concept of ancient history. Age-worn traditions were passing away. The critical method was applied to the scriptures. Some ministers went far beyond the scholars in casting doubt on the narratives of the Old Testament.

The records of the book of Genesis became the subject of fierce controversy. Doubt as to the historical value of the records spread from the Old Testament to the New. The Deity of Christ and the sacrificial nature of His death were denied.

Bishop Butler's description of the attitude of men toward religion has been applied to the period: "It has come, I know not how, to be taken for granted by many persons that Christianity is not so much a subject for inquiry but that it is now at length discovered to be fictitious." It was impossible for the clash of contending views to be post-poned indefinitely. The pulpit was charged with silent surrender to the radical betrayal of the evangelical foundations of the Christian faith.

Spurgeon's attitude was defined clearly. An eminent American once went into the tabernacle vestry and said, "Why, Mr. Spurgeon, you are preaching just what you preached twenty years ago when I was here."

"Yes, sir," was the response, "and if you come back in twenty years' time and hear me preach you will find me where I am now."

The controversy known as the "Down Grade" occurred over the years 1887 to 1892. It was not a squabble between Spurgeon and the Baptist Union; it was one of those thought conflicts which reappear in history when opposing ideas no longer can refuse battle. Spurgeon felt the challenge of the new ideas. The fact that he was a Baptist temporarily localized the area of controversy to the Baptist Union but it was one of those inevitable conflicts which profoundly affect all churches.

By 1887, Spurgeon had nothing to gain by entering into controversy. He was a sick man—indeed, he was marked for death. He had a great and unsullied reputation, with friends and admirers in all camps. Nothing less than an overwhelming duty to the faith he proclaimed and the Lord he honored could have sent him into the arena. Officials of county associations and ministers from all parts of the country appealed to him to raise his voice against the inroads of modernism.

He hated controversy and was not skillful at it. Though he held firmly to the Baptist position, he was at no time a strong denominationalist. To him, the fate of any union or denomination was nothing compared with preserving the truth. He perceived the general falling away from the evangelical position to be less in the Baptist Union than in other quarters but he felt that in his own denomination he should utter his greatest protest.

Spurgeon made three charges: 1) that the plenary inspiration of the scriptures was denied and thus the authority of the Bible was undermined, 2) that the vicarious nature of the death of Christ was not preached, and, therefore, the way of salvation was not made known and 3) that the doctrine of future punishment had given place to the idea of universal restoration and had weakened the motives for godly living.

In 1887, he was still on friendly terms with the Baptist Union. It was the year of Queen Victoria's jubilee. Members of the Baptist Board and their wives were entertained at the Stockwell Orphanage in May. Spurgeon was very genial and happy. He remarked that "in no body of ministers was there more brotherly love than among the Baptist ministers of London."

During the year, however, the Down Grade controversy began to loom large. The secretary of the union consulted Spurgeon in reference to the disturbing public utterances of two or three council members. These brethren were leaders, and what they said was reported in the press. The secretary, Dr. Booth, feared the union constitution provided no way by which the men could be called to account. He also feared the theology being taught in some of the colleges and its influence on students who soon would be in positions of responsibility.

A series of articles appeared in the *Sword and Trowel* lamenting the widespread declension from the faith. The author, Reverend R. Shindler, was defended by Spurgeon, who in the first of four articles wrote:

No lover of the gospel can conceal from himself the fact that the days are evil. We are willing to make a large discount from our apprehensions on the score of natural timidity, the caution of age, and the weakness produced by pain; but yet our solemn conviction is that things are much worse in many churches than they seem to be and are rapidly tending downward. Read those newspapers which represent the broad school of dissent, and ask yourself, How much farther could they go? What doctrine remains to be abandoned? What other truth to be the object of contempt? A new religion has been initiated, which is no more Christianity than chalk is cheese; and this religion, being destitute of moral honesty, palms itself off as the old faith with slight improvements, and on this plea usurps pulpits which were erected for gospel preaching.

Unfortunately, the articles in the *Sword and Trowel* appeared at the time journalists described as the "silly season." Editors ran short of interesting copy and gave great publicity to "the heresy hunt." A number of irresponsible writers added fuel to the fire.

Spurgeon called on the union for a declaration clearly stating the beliefs of the denomination. He did not want a collection of dogmatic pronouncements by which each member would be tested and judged but a straightforward statement to let the world know what Baptists stood for. Many letters passed between Spurgeon and Dr. Booth during the controversy.

In October 1887, Spurgeon felt there was nothing left for him but to withdraw from the union. He wrote his fateful letter to the secretary:

Dear Friend,

I beg to intimate to you as the secretary of the Baptist Union, that I must withdraw from that society. I do this with the utmost regret but I have no choice. The reasons are set forth in the Sword and Trowel *for November, and I trust you will excuse my repeating them here. I beg you not to send anyone to me to ask for a reconsideration. I fear I have considered too long already. Certainly every hour of the day impresses upon me the conviction that I am moving none too soon.*

I wish also to add that no personal pique or ill will in the least degree operated upon me. I have personally received more respect than I desire. It is on the highest ground alone that I take this step, and you know that I have delayed it because I hoped for better things.

Yours always heartily,
C. H. Spurgeon

This action caused consternation but not surprise. The London papers described it as "the breakup of the Baptist denomination" and saw in it "the decomposition of dissent."

In December the council of the Baptist Union met at the Mission House. It was claimed Spurgeon had never openly complained about a laxity of faith or practice, thus there was no justification for laying the matter before the full assembly. J. A. Spurgeon withdrew from the meeting in protest, and the breach was widened.

Spurgeon felt he was treated unfairly, and the injustice never was righted. The impression remained in many quarters that he had made charges which could not be substantiated, and when called on to produce his evidence he resigned and ran away. Nothing was further from the truth. He could have produced correspondence from Dr. Booth containing vital information but Booth considered it confidential. Spurgeon wrote in a letter to his wife: "For Dr. Booth to say I never complained is amazing. God knows all about it and He will see me righted."

The position was more than difficult. Spurgeon and Booth had been friends for many years. Both acted in good faith. Spurgeon had plenty of evidence. There were the utterances of well-known men which had been published in the *Christian World*, the *Independent*, the *Freeman*, the *British Weekly*, and the *Baptist*, proving Spurgeon's general charge.

Booth's policy was to keep silent in order not to widen the dispute. Meanwhile, Spurgeon everywhere was greeted enthusiastically. The Pastors' College Conference that year was one of the greatest in its history; at the annual supper a record thirty-seven hundred pounds was subscribed for college funds. Spurgeon received hundreds of letters, many of them from prominent people in all denominations. It was evident his action was largely approved.

The Baptist Union framed a resolution that was regarded as the basis for a reunion. Spurgeon was favorably impressed by it and hoped for the best. At the assembly of the union in April 1888, the council's resolution was hailed approvingly. It was regarded as the end of the controversy and a clear indication regarding the evangelical character of the assembly, though it declared "there is no need for additional tests of membership inasmuch as the council and the assembly have ample power under the constitution to determine all questions of membership and therefore to deal with the case of any church or person who may not hold evangelical doctrines."

The resolution was moved by the Reverend Charles

Williams in a speech hostile to Spurgeon. James Spurgeon "seconded the resolution but not the speech."

Spurgeon was disappointed. He wrote from Menton, "Those who write in the *Freeman* and the *Christian World* show how everything I do can be misconstrued, nevertheless I know what I have done and why I did it, and the Lord will bear me through."

The union proposed that several officials go to Menton immediately to deliberate with Spurgeon on how the unity of the denomination in truth, love, and good works might be maintained. Spurgeon declined, asking that the matter wait until he returned. His health gave cause for grave alarm. Even when he improved, his friends noted he had aged materially and moved slowly.

Spurgeon finally received union representatives in January 1889 but their task was fruitless. It was too late to reunite based on a resolution that already was interpreted in different ways. Spurgeon could not withdraw his resignation. When he was asked what he would advise to promote permanent unity, he answered, "Let the union have a simple basis of Bible truths. These are usually described as evangelical doctrines." He added that he knew no better summary of them than the one adopted by the Evangelical Alliance and followed by the members of many religious communities for several years. He did not brand the union as "a confederacy in evil." His words were: "It begins to look like a confederacy in evil."

The union council passed the following resolution when it received word of Spurgeon's refusal to withdraw his resignation:

(1) That the council deeply regrets the resignation of membership in the Union by the Reverend C. H.

Spurgeon, whose great gifts and usefulness are matters of joy and thankfulness to them and to the whole church of God. But, inasmuch as the conciliatory efforts of the deputation have been unavailing, the council has no alternative but to accept his resignation.

(2) That the council recognizes the gravity of the charges which Mr. Spurgeon has brought against the Union previous to and since his withdrawal. It considers that the public and general manner in which they have been made reflects on the whole body and exposes to suspicion brethren who love the truth as dearly as he does. And, as Mr. Spurgeon declines to give the names of those to whom he intended them to apply and the evidence supporting them, those charges, in the judgment of the council, ought not to have been made.

The Reverend James Douglas, MA, minister of Kenyon Chapel, Brixton, wrote:

While the Union cried, "Give us names," saying in effect, "We are in entire ignorance of your allegations," letters came to him from all parts of the country, bringing before him numerous cases of heretical teaching in the Baptist, Congregational, and other religious bodies. . . . Everything was not done in a corner. There were those who did not hesitate to declare themselves as rejectors of the gospel Mr. Spurgeon preached, and prominent attention had been called to these and kindred matters both in denominational print and in public assembly.

Two or three prominent members of the union declared themselves hostile to Spurgeon's views. The *Christian World*, in a leading article of November 3, 1887, had stated:

> *It is a plain and literal fact that those who share the opinions he condemns constitute a very large majority of all thinking Christian people.*

A strong case can be made for the Baptist Union. The majority of the council members knew nothing of the confidential communications between the secretary and Spurgeon. Dr. Booth no doubt believed until the last that Spurgeon would not withdraw. He depended on private conversations and was as afraid of publicity as of gunpowder.

Spurgeon endeavored to make it clear he had no personal feud. His references in public and private to his old friends showed that the bitterness of controversy had not soured the sweet memories of other days. There is no doubt, though, that he was deeply stung by the action of the Baptist Union and resented the suggestion that his statements were untrue.

Some of the Pastors' College men broke with their old leader. One or two indulged in attacks on "the new Pope." These men were very dear to the president, who must have felt as Caesar felt when Brutus joined the death plot.

It is impossible to tell how the Down Grade controversy might have gone had Spurgeon been healthy, or had the secretary of the Baptist Union supplied to the council the information he privately supplied to Spurgeon. The resolution, known as "the vote of censure" (though no censure was intended), made old friends enemies, or at least strangers, for the rest of their lives.

The healing hand of time may have closed the wounds

but Spurgeon's wound was never closed. He went on with his work, crowding the days with public engagements and new literary enterprises that might have provided work for half a dozen men. Yet he never recovered from the nervous strain of those terrible days.

In February 1888, the council adopted a declaration of principles commonly believed by the churches of the Union. Slightly amended, it was adopted April 21. It is sufficiently important to be presented as recorded:

> *While expressly disavowing and disallowing any power to control belief or to restrict inquiry, yet in view of the uneasiness produced in the churches by recent discussions and to show our agreement with one another and with our fellow Christians on the great truths of the gospel, the council deems it right to say that—*
>
> *(A) Baptized in the name of the Father, and of the Son, and of the Holy Ghost, we have avowed repentance toward God and faith in the Lord Jesus Christ—the very elements of a new life; as in the Supper we avow our union with one another, while partaking of the symbol of the body of our Lord, broken for us, and of the blood shed for the remission of sins. The Union, therefore, is an association of churches and ministers, professing not only to believe the facts and doctrines of the gospel but to have undergone the spiritual change expressed or implied in them. This change is the fundamental principle of our church life.*
>
> *(B) The following facts and doctrines are commonly believed by the churches of the Union:—*

1. *The divine inspiration and authority of the holy scripture as the supreme and sufficient rule of our faith and practice, and the right and duty of individual judgment in the interpretation of it.*
2. *The fallen and sinful state of man.*
3. *The Deity, the Incarnation, the Resurrection of the Lord Jesus Christ, and His sanctified and mediatorial work.*
4. *Justification by faith—a faith that works by love and produces holiness.*
5. *The work of the Holy Spirit in the conversion of sinners and in the sanctification of all who believe.*
6. *The Resurrection; the judgment at the Last Day, according to the words of our Lord in Matthew 25:46.*

To this last statement a footnote was added:

It should be stated, as a historical fact, that there have been brethren in the Union, working cordially with it, who, while reverently bowing to the authority of the holy scripture and rejecting the dogmas of purgatory and Universalism, have not held the common interpretation of these words of our Lord.

On the Baptist Union council were men whose evangelical teaching Spurgeon never doubted. Who could have questioned the teaching of James Culross, Alexander MacLaren, and a host of others who had stood by Spurgeon through all the years? They did not oppose him on any question of fidelity to the faith but rather on the issue of accepting an authoritative creed. They stood as Baptists ever stood, and as Spurgeon stood, for the supreme authority of our Lord Jesus Christ in all matters of religion.

His supporters spent many sleepless nights determining their loyalties. Should they follow their old chief, sharing his hope that "the day would come when in a larger communion than any sect can offer, all those who are one in Christ may be able to blend in manifest unity?" Or could they, though agreeing with the pastor against loose teaching, take their stand on the traditional Baptist position of opposition to authoritative creeds, liberty of prophesying, and the right of the local church to control its own ministry?

Baptists have had age-old hostility to authoritative creeds. Baptists stand for liberty, the right of each individual to receive the truth from the Lord. They know creeds often have been barriers to the free development of personality and have been used as instruments of persecution. Creeds have not secured uniformity of belief but have tended toward division and hypocrisy.

While at the beginning Spurgeon asked for a simple declaration of what the Baptist Union taught, some of his later utterances gave the impression he wanted a definite theological authority.

Spurgeon declared the question had been narrowed down to the truth or untruth of his statements but even that was a small matter compared to the sacred principles involved. Some of his students felt it their duty to tell their chief that they were remaining in the union, that while the protest was right, the procedure should be to contend for the faith within the union. Though he did not share their views, Spurgeon was affectionate and sympathetic and wanted them to remain in the Pastors' College Conference.

Most of Spurgeon's men remained in the Union—

Evangelicals who were wholeheartedly devoted to the great truths of the New Testament. When Spurgeon died, leaders of the Baptist Union without exception were loud in his praise. The Union passed a resolution that was one of the most eloquent tributes to the memory of the greatest Baptist the English pulpit has ever known.

FIFTEEN

The results of the Down Grade controversy were unspeakably trying to Spurgeon. He counted on much broader support than he received. Humiliated, he sincerely believed he had been betrayed.

In the spring of 1891 an influenza epidemic was ravaging London. Spurgeon continued his work, defying his own weakness. He preached some of his finest sermons—but the price had to be paid.

He had been driven to the conclusion that he needed another colleague in the tabernacle to fill the pulpit if necessary. The Reverend William Stott, whose work at St. John's Wood was well-known, accepted the invitation. Spurgeon said the addition was in case he collapsed just before or during a service, someone would be there to carry on. It was not long before Stott was carrying on.

On May 17, Spurgeon could not preach. He began the service and read part of the scripture, then turned to Stott and said, "Finish the reading." It was a dramatic moment.

Spurgeon seemed to stagger. Two deacons assisted him upstairs to his room. One of them quickly returned and announced that Spurgeon had an attack of giddiness and would be unable to continue the service. Stott offered prayer and asked for the sympathy of the people.

Spurgeon was permitted to speak on the morning of June 7. His text was 1 Samuel 30:21–25. The sermon was published as No. 2,208 in the regular weekly series, titled "The Statute of David for the Sharing of the Spoil." That was his last utterance on the platform which for more than thirty years had been his pulpit throne. An estimated twenty million people had attended his services during that period.

His last words were spoken in the usual hush of almost awe-inspiring attention. Very quietly he said:

> *If you wear the livery of Christ, you will find Him so meek and lowly of heart that you will find rest unto your souls. He is the most magnanimous of captains. There never was His like among the choicest of princes. He is always to be found in the thickest part of the battle. When the wind blows cold He always takes the bleak side of the hill. The heaviest end of the cross lies on His shoulders. If He bids us carry a burden, He carries it, also. If there is anything that is gracious, generous, kind and tender, yea, lavish and superabundant in love, you always find it is Him. His service is life, peace, joy. Oh, that you would enter it at once! God help you to enlist under the banner of Jesus Christ!*

On the following Friday Spurgeon was stricken down with serious symptoms. Prayer meetings were held all day. Letters and telegrams came from all over the country. The chief rabbi, Gladstone, the archbishop of Canterbury, and the highest persons in the land inquired.

In September Spurgeon was moved to Eastbourne, and he returned in October, jubilant at the prospect of renewing his work. But it was not to be. It was deemed necessary to take him, an invalid, to the south of France. Menton had worked wonders for him before, and he dreamed of the time he would come back to his beloved place in the tabernacle. He was very happy at the thought that his wife would be his companion on this trip to Menton. Mrs. Spurgeon had been a prisoner of pain for many years but this time his beloved "Susie" was well enough to be at his side.

The fateful journey began October 26. The Spurgeons were accompanied by Dr. and Mrs. J. A. Spurgeon, Mr. Harrald, and Mr. Allison. The trip was uneventful. The passing of stations on the road recalled memories of other days and pilgrimages in search of strength. Health had been found then; why should it not be repeated?

Spurgeon loved the fair land of France second only to England. French history gave him many illustrations and much pleasure. He regarded Napoleon as one of the great men of destiny. Carlyle's *French Revolution* was a favorite work he had read several times and seemed never tired of quoting.

At Menton, from the unpretentious hotel that had become his home, was a view of loveliness. He would sit by the window in eloquent stillness that made the noise of London seem foolish, controversies senseless. There he often had found the balm of healing strengthen his soul. Even in pain, he often could forget the body in the sheer joy of scenic beauty. He knew the valley of the shadow but was far more familiar with the sunshine on the hills and enjoyed it fully.

His condition varied almost daily. He had little doubt he would return to the tabernacle and continue his ministry for years to come. He thought of the pruning of the vine, that it might bear richer fruit.

The correspondence he dictated to his secretary indicated the changing barometer. Early in November he wrote:

The story of my cure has been very marvelous, and this last part of it is all of a piece with the rest. My brother, whose care has made the journey less formidable, when he returns, will have a cheering tale to tell of me and my dear wife whose presence with me makes every single enjoyment into seven.

Later he said:

To go up a few steps, to take a short walk, to move a parcel, and all such trifles become a difficulty, so that Solomon's words are true: "The grasshopper is a burden." I think I could preach but when I have seen a friend for five minutes I begin to feel that I have done as much speaking as I can well manage.

A week later he reported:

I feel I shall get better but one thing is forced upon my mind, that I am weak as water and that building up is slower work than pulling down.

Spurgeon wrote to his friend Holden Pike, asking for an article on the flower girls of London. In December he wrote to his beloved family at the orphanage:

Dear Boys and Girls,

I send you all my love so far as the postman can carry it at 2´d. for half an ounce. I wish you a real glorious Christmas; I might have said "a jolly Christmas" if we had all been boys but as some of us are girls I will be proper and say "a merry Christmas." Enjoy yourselves and be grateful to the kind friends who will find money to keep the Stockwell Orphanage supplied. Bless their loving hearts, they never let you want for anything. May they have pleasure in seeing you all grow up to be good men and women. . . . I should like you to have a fine day, such a day as we have here but if not, you will be warm and bright indoors. Three cheers for those who give us the good things for this festival. I want you for a moment in the day to be still and to spend the time in thanking our Heavenly Father and the Lord Jesus Christ for great goodness shown to you and to me, and then to pray that I may get quite well.

Later he wrote to the church. Hopes and fears fought for the victory. Many were quite sure his life would be spared; they could not believe God would allow His servant to pass away at a time when he seemed needed desperately. The controversy had quieted down; there was a truce of God but the forces still were armed for battle. Away in the quiet, the sufferer tried to forget and did his best to assist nature's healing ministry by cultivating a tranquil mind.

A year before, Spurgeon had preached the opening sermon at the new Presbyterian church at Menton. He was anxious to attend service there again but it was not to be.

Loving care did everything possible during the next three months, and messages of inquiry and comfort came from all over the world. He was glad his wife was with him to enjoy the land of sunshine and flowers. The rooms in the Hitel Beau Rivage, which had been reserved for his party year by year, were more cheerful. After awhile, as in former years, little parties gathered for morning worship. Sometimes Spurgeon himself was able to read the scripture or offer prayer but the effort was too much. He tried to continue his exposition of the gospel of Matthew and articles for the *Sword and Trowel*. He and his friends often were deceived by an appearance of health, while the deadly disease spread.

The sunshine was a great delight; he almost lived in the open air. His favorite route was around the Boulevard Victoria and along the breakwater. He always admired the view of the old town across the harbor.

January 10 and 17 were memorable. He decided to hold a little service for his friends. He called it "breaking the long silence." The company came to his sitting room. He was persuaded not to try a new address but to read them part of his exposition of Matthew.

Prebendary Wilson Carlile wrote to me:

> *When he was dying at the East Bay, Menton, my wife and I went to his family prayers which he took though in bed. He prayed for all wandering sheep, concluding, "Thou, Lord, seest the various labels upon them and rightly regardest them by the mark of the cross in their hearts. They are all Thy one fold."*

At these little services in his private room, representatives of all the denominations were welcome. Years before, it had been Spurgeon's custom to hold a Communion service that was open to any who wished to unite. He made his position clear:

Dear to our hearts is that great article of the Apostles' Creed: "I believe in the Communion of saints." I believe not in the Communion of Episcopalians alone; I do not believe in the Communion of Baptists only; I dare not sit with them exclusively; I think I should be almost strict Communionist enough not to sit with them at all, because I should say: "This is not the Communion of saints, it is the Communion of Baptists." Whosoever loves the Lord Jesus Christ in sincerity and truth hath a hearty welcome and is not only permitted but invited to commune with the Church of Christ.

At the January 17 service, before offering the final prayer in the last service in which he took part on earth, Spurgeon announced they would sing one of his favorite hymns. It was the well-known "The Sands of Time Are Sinking." The last verse:

*I've wrestled on towards heaven
'Gainst storm and wind and tide.
Now like a weary traveler
That leaneth on his guide,
Amid the shades of evening
While sinks life's lingering sand
I hail the glory dawning
From Immanuel's land.*

Thank-Offering Day at the tabernacle in London was held on Tuesday. A telegram was received from the pastor: "Self and wife one hundred pounds hearty thank-offering toward tabernacle general expenses. Love to all friends."

That was Spurgeon's last gift—indeed, his last message.

Soon afterward he became unconscious and remained so until the following Sunday. Just after eleven at night he left those who had accompanied him to the riverside and passed through the deep waters alone, except for the One who never forsakes those who put their trust in Him.

The little company could hardly realize the spirit of "Mr. Valiant for Truth" had really departed but on the other side the sound of trumpets was heard. Messages of sympathy came in shoals. The most exalted persons in the land were among the first to send consolation.

The casket containing all that was mortal bore the inscription: "In ever loving memory of Charles Haddon Spurgeon, born at Kelvedon, June 19, 1834, fell asleep in Jesus at Menton, January 31, 1892. I have fought a good fight, I have finished my course, I have kept the faith."

Spurgeon had decided his burial site would be the grounds of the Stockwell Orphanage. "Many would come to look at the grave and then would help the orphans in whom he took so deep an interest." But that was made impossible by the South London Electric Railway, so he decided on Norwood Cemetery, where hundreds of his friends and church members were laid to rest.

Shortly before his death he had whispered to his secretary, "Remember, a plain stone. 'C.H.S.' and no more; no fuss." Undoubtedly he had in mind the plain slab over John Calvin's grave in Geneva with its two letters: "J.C."

Spurgeon's tomb was marked by a modest memorial erected by church officers. But those who seek Spurgeon's monument will not find it at Norwood. It is living in the hearts of thousands of men and women all over the world. It is found in the tabernacle. During his long pastorate, no fewer than 14,691 people were received into fellowship. At his death, the roll contained 5,311 names; there were twenty-two mission stations, twenty-seven Sunday and "ragged" schools with 312 teachers and 8,034 scholars.

Though by no means a lover of controversy, Spurgeon was a valiant fighter. He never whined or cried that he might be spared. He stood and took the consequences. But there comes a time when the body is too weak for the battlefield, the brain too tired.

There have been many warriors who have fought the good fight, finished their course, and kept the faith. Each received the "Well done, good and faithful servant." But the Christian church has only one Spurgeon. He was God's greatest gift to the modern church. His life is a trumpet call to the timid and fearful. Though dead, he still proclaims the message that lives and will live forever.

It is fitting that the tired warrior closed his eyes amid scenes he loved so well. Could he have chosen, he would have died on the field.

SIXTEEN

I t is generally supposed the mystic and the man of action stand in contrast but a wiser view reveals that the dreamers are the doers. The real mystics were not those who withdrew from the dusty road of life to spend their years in uninterrupted meditation of the unseen. Spurgeon was supremely a man of affairs, a sturdy Protestant. "Dream stuff" had no place in his philosophy—but what a dreamer he was.

Too often mysticism has been identified with a wild symbolism that attempts to discover allegories of spiritual things in all earthly events. The old mystics would have maintained that all life may be regarded as analogical, dimly hinting at the form of the hidden reality.

Christian mystics are those who believe in spiritual mysteries and claim it is possible to enter into a fellowship with God which lifts the soul into another region of experience. A mystery is necessarily something that cannot be fully understood but not necessarily something that cannot be shared and enjoyed. The secret hidden from the wise and prudent may be revealed to babes. They may obtain it, though they could never explain it. Benjamin Jowett in his introduction to Plato's *Phaedrus* wrote:

> *By mysticism we mean not the extravagance of an erring fancy but the concentration of reason in feeling, enthusiastic love of the good, the true, the one; the sense of the infinity of knowledge and of the marvel of the human faculties.*

Christian mysticism stands for the initiation into fuller and deeper knowledge of Divine things, by which the spirit is led toward ultimate union with God. It represents such a union between Christ and the soul that nothing can come between. Some mystics have no evangelical sympathies; others are natural mystics, represented by Emerson, to whom religion seems to involve some sort of pantheism.

Spurgeon often described what the mystics would have called "the experience of the dark night of the soul." In the first volume of *The New Park Street Pulpit* is an amazing sermon on "The Desire of the Soul in Spiritual Darkness." It was preached June 24, 1855, based on the text: "With my soul have I desired Thee in the night." Describing the darkness that may fall on the believer, the preacher said:

> *At certain periods clouds and darkness cover the sun, and he [the believer] beholds no clear shining of the daylight but walks in darkness. Now there are many who have rejoiced in the presence of God for a season; they have basked in the sunshine God has been pleased to give them in the earlier stages of their Christian career; they have walked along the "green pastures," by the side of the "still waters," and*

suddenly—in a month or two—they find that glorious sky is clouded; instead of "green pastures," they have to tread the sandy desert; in the place of "still waters," they find streams brackish to their taste and bitter to their spirits, and they say, "Surely, if I were a child of God this would not happen." Oh! say not so, thou who art walking in darkness. The best of God's saints have their nights; the dearest of His children have to walk through a weary wilderness. There is not a Christian who has enjoyed perpetual happiness; there is no believer who can always sing a song of joy. It is not every lark that can always carol. It is not every star that can always be seen. And not every Christian is always happy. Perhaps the King of Saints gave you a season of great joy at first because you were a raw recruit, and He would not put you into the roughest part of the battle when you had first enlisted. You were a tender plant, and He nursed you in the hothouse till you could stand the severe weather. You were a young child, and therefore He wrapped you in furs and clothed you in the softest mantle. But now you have become strong, and the case is different. Capuan holidays do not suit Roman soldiers; and they would not agree with Christians. We need clouds and darkness to exercise our faith; to cut off self-dependence and make us put more faith in Christ and less in evidence, less in experience, less in frames and feelings.

Very early in his Christian experience, Spurgeon described the utter darkness of the soul that settled upon him, leading him to doubt everything. Pilgrims who can ascend the hill of the Lord also can descend into the valley of the shadow. Spurgeon knew the heights and the depths—heights so exalted they were in the uninterrupted sunshine of the divine Presence, and depths so deep there was no light at all. He understood the experience of unsparing self-abandonment to God.

> *Therefore bear in mind, beloved, no works of ours, no merit of ours, have any value in the eyes of God—for all is of grace, and all the merit is that of the Lord Jesus, flowing not from us to God but from God to us.*
>
> *By this way and by this alone have all the saints drawn near to God. How much might I not say of the cross of Christ, and yet never could any man say enough; for it is far beyond the mind of the high angels to understand how the eternal God in His great love became a man and suffered the deepest shame and the bitterest sorrow for us.*

So preached John Tauler in Strasbourg in 1340. The preacher might have been Spurgeon. Many of Spurgeon's passages contain not only the same faith but almost the same phrasing.

The great mystics did not spend their time simply nursing the sickness of the soul. We find them undertaking missionary journeys under conditions which might well appall perfectly healthy people. We find them organizing and reforming religious orders, managing large hospitals, administering public funds, leading great movements, and doing all these things with practical acumen and success. There is nothing vague and dreamy, nothing occult and creepy about them.

Paul said, "I will come to visions and revelations of the

Lord." He told of a man—perhaps himself—who was caught up to the third heaven and heard unspeakable words unlawful for a human to utter. The "great commission" calling to the vocation was received in moments of vision. The voice spoke to Moses at the burning bush. The Hebrew prophets dreamed strange dreams. Our Lord Himself heard the voice at His baptism. All through the ages people have heard the voice: "Whom shall I send, and who will go for us?"

From the earliest days Spurgeon knew the delights of intimate communion with his Lord. In a sermon full of tender beauty, he described Christ manifesting Himself to His people:

I know what some would say. They would cry, "Nonsense, we believe religion is a thing very good, to keep people in order but as to these manifestations and these ecstasies, we do not believe in them." Very well, beloved, I have proved the truth of what the text says. He does not manifest Himself unto the world. You have proved yourselves that you are of the world because you have not any manifestations.

If I were to go much further I should be accused of fanaticism, and so it may be; but yet I will believe and must believe that there are seasons when the Christian lives next door to heaven. If I had not gone within an inch of the pearly gates I am not here; if I have not sometimes sniffed the incense from the censers of the glorified and heard the music of their harps, I think I am not a living man. There have been seasons of ecstatic joy, when I have climbed the highest mountains, and I have caught some sweet whisper from the throne. Have you had such manifestations? I will not condemn you if you

*have not. But I believe most Christians have them,
and if they are much in duty and much in suffering,
they will have them. It is not given to all to have
that portion but to some it is, and such men know
what religion means.*

*I was reading a short time ago of a Mr. Ten-
nant. He was about to preach one evening and
thought he would take a walk. As he was walking in
a wood, he felt so overpoweringly the presence of
Christ and such a manifestation of Him that he
knelt down, and they could not discover him at the
hour when he was to have preached. He continued
there for hours, insensible as to whether he was in
the body or out of the body; and when they waked
him he looked like a man who had been with Jesus,
and whose face shone. He never should forget, he
said, to his dying day, that season of communion,
when positively, though he could not see Christ,
Christ was there, holding fellowship with him, heart
against heart, in the sweetest manner. A wondrous
display it must have been. You must know something
of it, if not much; otherwise you have not gone far
on your spiritual course. God teach you more and
lead you deeper!*

Spurgeon never lost his mysticism. While laboring or
traveling, he delighted in the beautiful vision. Whenever he
spoke to his Savior, he lingered with the longing of love to
see more, so he might tell more. His one passion was Christ.
He reveled in spiritualizing Solomon's Song. In a sermon on
"Heavenly Lovesickness," he described the longing of the
soul to come closer and closer to the Lord:

You know how sweet it was in the past. Beloved, what times we have had, some of us. Oh, whether in the body or out of the body we cannot tell—God knoweth. What mountings! Talk ye of eagles' wings—they are earthly pinions and may not be compared with the wings with which He carried us up from earth. Speak of mounting beyond clouds and stars!—they were left far, far behind. We entered into the unseen, beheld the invisible, lived in the immortal, drank in the ineffable, and were blessed with the fullness of God in Christ Jesus, being made to sit together in heavenly places in Him. Well, all this is to come again: "I will see you again, and your heart shall rejoice." "A little while, and ye shall not see me: and again, a little while, and ye shall see me." "In a little wrath I hid my face from thee for a moment: but with everlasting kindness will I have mercy on thee, saith the Lord thy Redeemer." Think of this. Why, we have comfort even in this sickness of love. Our heart, though sick, is still whole, while we are panting and pining after the Lord Jesus.

The true motive of the mystic is the love which desires not the benevolence of God but God Himself, the love which cannot rest until it rests in the Lord. It rejoices that all love has its source in the love that passeth knowledge. It cries with one of old: "Let me love or not live."

Spurgeon's mysticism did not lead him away from the solid earth. While in spirit he loved to linger at the foot of the cross, he did not leave any duty undone. He was not blind to the needs of the ignorant and the poor; he was not deaf to the cries of fatherless children. The soul becomes more sensitive as it learns to wait on the Lord. God calls His children to be Christlike; they are saved for service not for themselves alone.

One of Spurgeon's outstanding characteristics was his absolute confidence in God. He believed without qualification that the Lord Jesus Christ not only saved from the penalty and power of sin but that He was the ever-present Friend, keeping the promise He made to the disciples that He would be with them always, even to the end of the age. The glad certainty was never quite absent, even in the darkest hours of Spurgeon's suffering and conflict, He knew he was not alone. And he insisted it was within the reach of any human to know Christ and enjoy the unspeakable preciousness of the Presence.

Spurgeon contended Christ was not simply an ideally beautiful character who made men good by His influence. He proclaimed Christ the Son of God, the historical and spiritual reality, the abiding Presence made known to all who tread the mystic path. All that Christ did in the days of His flesh, He still is doing in our midst. Spurgeon knew people would not continue to worship and love any character who was no more than a dream. He loved to see the way Christ worked through the preaching of the gospel. The life-changing preachers had different names but they all bore testimony to the power by which the change is wrought.

Sometimes Spurgeon loved to browse in Romans, finding food for the soul. He lingered over the declarations concerning those for whom "there is therefore now no condemnation." He frequently quoted the great words with which the eighth chapter concluded:

> *Who shall separate us from the love of Christ? shall tribulation, or distress, or persecution, or famine, or nakedness, or peril, or sword? As it is written, For*

thy sake we are killed all the day long; we are accounted as sheep for the slaughter. Nay, in all these things we are more than conquerors through him that loved us. For I am persuaded, that neither death, nor life, nor angels, nor principalities, nor powers, nor things present, nor things to come, nor height, nor depth, nor any other creature, shall be able to separate us from the love of God, which is in Christ Jesus our Lord.

The mystic bond unites all true disciples. They know Him and they know each other. Spurgeon taught:

Here is the power to promote the union of the people of God. There is a man there, he is almost a Puseyite. "I do not like him," says one. Stop till I tell you something more about him, and you will. There is another man there, a Presbyterian—true blue; he cannot bear Independency or anything but Presbytery—a covenant man. "Well," says one, "I like him a little better but I do not suppose we shall get on very well." Stop! I will tell you some more about him. There is another man down there; he is a very strong Calvinist. "Humph," says one, "I shall not admire him." Stop, stop! Now here are these three men; let us hear what they say of each other. If they know nothing of each other except what I have stated, the first time they meet there will be a magnificent quarrel. There is yonder clergyman—he will have little fraternity whatever with the ultra-Evangelical, while the Presbyterian will reject them both, for he abhors black prelacy.

But, my dear brethren, all three of you, we of

this congregation will approve of you all, and you will approve of one another when I have stated your true character. That man yonder, whom I called almost a Puseyite, was George Herbert. How he loved the doornails of the church! I think he would scarce have had a spider killed that had once crept across the church aisles. He was a thorough churchman, to the very center of the marrow of his bones but what a Christian! What a lover of his sweet Lord Jesus! You know that hymn of his which I have so often quoted and mean to quote a hundred times more: "How sweetly doth 'My Master' sound," and so forth. I hear a knock at the door. "Who is that?" "Why, it is a very strong churchman." "Do not show him in; I am at prayer: I cannot pray with him." "Oh but it is George Herbert!" "Oh, let him in! No man could I pray better with than Mr. Herbert. Walk in, Mr. Herbert; we are right glad to see you; you are our dear companion; your hymns have made us glad."

But who was that second man, the Presbyterian, who would not have liked George Herbert at all? Why, that was Samuel Rutherford. What a seraphic spirit! What splendid metaphors he uses about his sweet Lord Jesus! He has written all Solomon's Song over without knowing it. He felt and proved it to be divine. The Spirit in him redictated the song. Well now, I think we will introduce Mr. Rutherford and Mr. Herbert together, and I am persuaded when they begin to speak about their Master they will find each other next of kin; and I feel sure that, by this time, Samuel Rutherford and George Herbert have found each other out in heaven and are sitting side by side.

Well, but then we mentioned another; who was that High Calvinist? He was the man who was called the leviathan of Antinomians. That he was a leviathan I will grant but that he was an Antinomian is false. It was Dr. Hawker. Now I am sure George Herbert would not have liked Dr. Hawker, and I am certain that Dr. Hawker would not have liked George Herbert, and I do not suppose that Samuel Rutherford would have had anything to do with either of them. "No, no," he would say, "your black prelacy I hate." But look at Hawker; there is a sweet spirit; he cannot take up his pen but he dips it in Christ and begins to write about his Lord at once. "Precious Immanuel—precious Jesus." Those words in his morning and evening portions are repeated again and again and again. I recollect hearing of Mr. Rowland Hill, that he said to a young man who was at tea with him one night when he was about to go: "Where are you going to?" "Oh!" said he, "I am going to hear Dr. Hawker, at St. George's in the borough." "Oh, go and hear him," he said; "he is a right good man, worth hearing. But there is a difference between him and me; my preaching is something like a pudding, with here and there a plum; but Dr. Hawker's is all plum." And that was very near the mark, because Dr. Hawker was all Christ. He was constantly preaching of his Master; and even if he gave an invitation to a sinner, it was generally put in this way: "What sayest thou? Wilt thou go with this man and be married and espoused unto him?" It was the preaching of a personal Christ that made his ministry so full of marrow and fatness.

My dear friends, let a man stand up and exalt Christ, and we are all agreed. I see before me this afternoon members of all Christian denominations; but if Christ Jesus is not the topic that suits you, why then I think we may question your Christianity. The more Christ is preached, the more will the church prove, and exhibit, and assert, and maintain her unity; but the less Christ is preached, and the more of Paul, and Apollos, and Cephas, the more of strife and division, and the less of true Christian fellowship.

Spurgeon was more Catholic than the Roman Catholic Church itself. He knew there was a unity of substance in Christian experience, though it might be expressed in a variety of systems. The Friend had many friends with different names, just as the Good Shepherd had other sheep not of this fold. Christians disagree in theology but in spiritual fellowship they are wonderfully alike. Sturdy Protestants have no difficulty singing hymns composed by the early Catholic fathers; the authorship does not interfere with the devotion with which the lines are sung. Spurgeon loved to think all who named the name of Christ and found in Him their Master would come to the same goal: the Father's house at last.

Spurgeon's services were magnificent and many-sided but much of the message was temporary, passing with the circumstances it called forth. Some of it was controversial, dealing with topics that leave the modern mind puzzled but not interested. Perhaps his most important contribution will turn out to be the spiritual enrichment of the life of the time—and all times—found in the eternal truth of God. His evidence is the message of all the mystics who have known the Christ.

Is this not a message of hope for the present? When

religious leadership is not quite sure which way to go, when many pilgrims honestly confess that they walk alone without inner light or guidance, it is important to recapture the clarion tones of that matchless voice, sincere and sure, concerning the deepest needs of the soul.

Now that the sense of security in this life and the life to come has been shaken rudely, the old sanctities put aside, the authorities discounted, it is good to listen again to the great apostle of experience who found the way and followed it, whose shrewd practical wisdom stood the test of time. Here was a witness who spoke what he knew and told of things of which he was certain. Here was reality. Here was a modern saint who embodied the gospel in a great message and worked it out in a greater benediction.

Christ's cross and presence were the delights of Spurgeon's life. He always loved to point to Christ crucified. The proof of his gospel was in the works it enabled him to accomplish.

SEVENTEEN

What makes C. H. Spurgeon of value in our time? What gives permanent value to any character?

A personality that mirrors the life of the times is always of value. Some novelists become permanent through their pictorial treatment of their age. Other people become memorable by the influence made on the thought of their time and the changes they bring in their own day and for generations to come. There may be other reasons but these seem essential.

The religious conflicts of the last half of the Victorian era were fought out in Spurgeon's lifetime. The materialism of science and philosophy challenged all beliefs dear to the heart and reduced the conception of faith to an attempt to believe that which one knew was not true.

The churches were at a crossroads, uncertain of the way. Calvinism was more rigid than Calvin's own teaching and was discounted; its doctrine of man destroyed any real sense of moral responsibility and left the creature the victim of fate. Spurgeon taught the sovereignty of God and built his theology on God's immovable character. He quickly set aside hyper-Calvinism and, during the greater part of his ministry, was under attack from that direction.

Spurgeon's doctrine—humans' power to choose—laid him open to attack from theologians who did not believe in free will and from the advocates of scientific philosophy who expounded a newfound solution for the old problems of the universe and launched a new attack on religion. Spurgeon found pulpit gladiators facing him with all the weapons they could command.

The new philosophers regarded Darwin as another Moses. There was no room in their philosophy for anything but cause and effect. The color of the rose, the poetry of Milton, and the tragedy in Shakespeare's mind were all products of physical causes. The new philosophy brought a sense of irresponsibility and a general cheapening of life.

Spurgeon appealed to the moral conscience of humans. And his good news was not for a type or class but for all.

Could this gospel he taught have rekindled hope in the hearts of thousands of people who were ready to give up in despair? Spurgeon's Calvinism was such that while he preached the majesty of God, he ascribed freedom of will to humans and insisted anyone might find deliverance from sin's power in Jesus. In an age of doubt, he taught that the sky might be radiant with hope and the outlook more beautiful than the loveliest landscape. Humans united with Christ could ascend to the throne of heaven.

One of the terrible legacies of the Victorian pulpit was the suspicion of insincerity. Preachers did not tell lies but they did not tell quite all they believed or knew. Stopford Brooke made a great contribution to the mid-Victorian pulpit by refusing to retain his position in the Established Church when he had ceased to believe its creeds. He may have been entirely wrong in his judgment but he was entirely right in refusing to preach what he believed was erroneous.

Spurgeon's thorough sincerity commanded the respect of many who did not accept his views. There was never a doubt about his honor and truth. He was indignant with preachers who failed to declare "the whole counsel of God." In the dark days of the Down Grade controversy, he contended that preachers were withholding their own views, that to be consistent they should leave the pulpit and find a platform where they would be free.

The fundamental character of his thinking rendered good service. He sought to get to the core of true religion. He was not content to lead people to the outer courts of the temple; he guided them inside, so they would realize they were all priests of God. His latter sermons show his anxiety to unveil the mysteries, to get behind the metaphors and allegories to the basic truths.

Spurgeon had no easy method of solving life's problems. He was not superficial. While others scraped the surface, he sought to penetrate to the depths.

It may be that the age of great men was passing, that preachers, like politicians and writers, were not attaining the standards of their predecessors. Spurgeon was described as "the last of the Puritans." Puritanism in the narrow sense was simply a designation of seventeenth-century dissent from the Church of England. Ironically, it was the creed of the killjoys—but it was more than a point of view. Spurgeon embodied Puritanism as it is represented in theology. He also embodied that Puritanism which, as a way of life, stood for fidelity to the ideals of clean-mindedness.

Spurgeon may be described as the first of the "new Puritans." He certainly was not the last of his type. Puritanism is not simply a question of opposition to this or that; it is a spirit rather than a formula. Spurgeon's Puritanism did not create artificial sins or add to the Ten Commandments. It was expressed in joyous laughter. It was eminently a religion for humans. One characteristic of the tabernacle congregation was the large proportion of young people obviously enjoying their religion.

Yet the religion that was "brief, bright, and brotherly," not knowing the stern side of truth, was not Spurgeon's faith. He took violated justice and outraged love seriously and knew that, after all, there is something of which wrongdoers must reasonably be afraid.

He did not spare the enemies of the faith. He made strong, stinging comments. He did not sullenly oppose modern thought but the new liberalism, in his judgment, was tampering with the moral sense of the people and sapping the spiritual life of the church.

Spurgeon taught the confused and overwrought that life was intended to be music, not discord. Humans should be at peace. No power, human or satanic, could destroy the tranquility of the soul in union with Jesus Christ.

He taught that freedom came in submission to the highest authority, that liberty was never license, that anarchy means chaos. He said:

> *Christ has conquered for us. We share His victory. When He began with us we were but a prey to diverse lusts and evil powers. Satan ruled us, the world rode roughshod over us; we were evil.*

How wonderfully Spurgeon appealed to the moral sense. How dramatically he represented the conflict of the opposing wills in one personality. His was a message of hope to the individual, never more needed than in our time. With his wealth of metaphors and illustrations, he set forth the conquest of Christ over individuals, so that our desires become the expression of the Divine decree. Spurgeon insisted truth and holiness were "two sides of one penny." Whatever happened, he would not lower the ideal or agree to the fatal separation. There may be morality without religion but there cannot be Christianity without morality.

Spurgeon stood like a rock against the incoming tide of modernism. He served the new generation by keeping his feet on solid foundations. He kept in touch with reality, hating all that was artificial or obscure, approaching the world's problems in plain language, not shrinking from the humiliation of confessing that he had no solution to many of the problems.

He played no tricks with his great public—though it might have been easy, given his matchless dramatic power, to gain the mind's consent by appealing to the heart. When he appealed to the emotions, he did so frankly and without apology. But generally, there was very little emotionalism in his preaching. He paid his congregation the compliment of appealing to their intelligence.

In the pulpit, as in private life, Spurgeon displayed a shrewd wit, sweetened by tender sympathy and enlivened by irresistible humor. But he always kept in close touch with honesty. He would not teach with reservations. He told the truth as he knew it. Often it was unpleasant but those who listened knew he was sincere.

Spurgeon was not blind to human weakness. He knew the infirmities of the flesh and the passions of manhood. But he knew something more, and that enabled him to stand firm, recognizing humans are not victims but victors. One of his favorite quotations was: "Work out your own salvation in fear and trembling. For it is God which worketh in you both to will and to do of his own good pleasure."

While the tabernacle congregation included men and women of position and wealth, the great majority of worshipers struggled daily. They knew the sordid side of existence. Some found it difficult to pay for their family's daily bread. The more fortunate belonged to the middle class: skilled artisans, clerks, and keepers of small shops. For most, life was drab and gray. The tabernacle service was almost their only pleasure; there, they found a little breathing space where they could look with unhurried eyes upon the King in His beauty.

It is no small achievement that Spurgeon kept his vision unclouded and his optimism undaunted. Even at the end of the journey, when he described himself as "under the weather," he returned continually to the message of hope. It was the period during which the new teaching of the scientists was filtering through the public mind. The note of pessimism grew louder, and Spurgeon—a martyr to pain and controversy—would have been less than human had he not felt the chill of human skepticism. He found courage in his unshaken belief in the sovereignty of God and the Divine decree that the golden age would dawn in Christ. He was the knight-errant of the Kingdom of God, leading lost humans to believe in the Promised Land.

Rumor said Spurgeon would die a very wealthy man but rumor was disappointed. At the tabernacle, he never appealed for money without giving a subscription to the fund, and frequently he was the largest subscriber. The attitude toward money is an acid test of religion. Spurgeon's judgment sometimes may have been mistaken but his honesty was never questioned.

Spurgeon's world was weakened by the pursuit of

pleasure and drugged by despair. There were increasing signs of the passing of the creeds and standards that had seemed so firmly planted in religious life. It was not surprising that he sometimes felt alone. In these moods, it would have been impossible to realize the inspiration of faith, had there not been personal sincerity.

Spurgeon had not chosen his vocation, though he loved it with all the passion of a bridegroom's affection. He realized he was called by God to be what he was.

He bore a heavy handicap. Essentially a countryman, it seemed hardly likely he could understand the mind of city dwellers. He was a son of the soil; the fragrance of the haystack was a great delight. All his tastes were with nature, the far-stretching lands and open heavens. In a city, would he not be like a bird in a cage? London filled him with something like fear, and only the urge of destiny turned his feet toward the metropolis.

The difficulties of his own nature were considerable. His genius was undisciplined and hardly understood by himself. He was naturally impulsive and explosive, quick to see and to speak, with an independent spirit that would accept no patronage. The churches were surprised and almost shocked by him; the ministers mildly amused and critical; the press sarcastic, holding him up to ridicule; the public fearful of pulpit mountebanks.

Spurgeon faced his difficulties with supreme confidence in God and his mission. By sheer hard work he gained the people's ear, winning the confidence of churches and ministers. It was not by genius alone that he came to the pulpit throne. Those who knew him recognized the labor of the servant as well as the Master's blessing.

Just as Spurgeon would not excuse himself from labor, neither would he excuse others. He could be very angry with students who tried to shuffle out of their studies. Said John Ploughman:

My advice to my boys has been get out of the slug-gard's way or you may catch his disease and never get rid of it. I am always afraid of their learning the ways of the idle and am very watchful to nip any-thing of the sort in the bud.

He showed preachers the value of the direct method. A favorite attitude of his when preaching was to stand upright with head thrown back, the left hand grasping the rail of the platform and the right arm extended with the index finger pointing. He loved direct simplicity. Simplicity of thought and speech were not the chief characteristics of his time. Many preachers made simple truths complex. As Spurgeon said, "They love to go on the roundabout."

The Authorized Version of the English Bible was his standard and court of appeal. Though thoroughly conservative in his outlook, he did not hesitate to use any help that came from modern scholarship. His mind was not hospitable to theological speculation and wavering attitudes. He planted himself unreservedly on the Bible as he understood it.

If Spurgeon could return to London today, he hardly would recognize it. The world, the flesh, and the devil appear in other forms but they do not disappear. Would Spurgeon become bewildered in this new world? The almost endless rush of traffic and people leave no place for meditation. He would face competitors unknown in his day. Today's media make the old-fashioned service terribly dull. In his day there were no star preachers on radio and television who could be switched off if they became uninteresting.

Each generation produces a new company of worshipers, not quite the same type as their predecessors. Modern congregations no longer look to the pulpit with unquestioning eyes. People have lost their power to sit and concentrate for an hour or so on a complex subject. They have little inclination to follow theological reasoning—or any other reasoning. There is a lust for change and variety.

What could Spurgeon do under our changed conditions? Certainly he would not settle down to the conventional methods and accept defeat. He would explore fresh approaches to the masses. But he would not minimize the difficulties. "The church should be used to dying," he said. "Does she not die to live?"

That is the hope of the future.

Christian history is a good tonic for the depressed. Whenever the evangelist for the age has spoken, the hosts of waiting souls have recognized the call and rallied to the cross. Any day, the voice may be heard and the miracle happen. People are not educated into Christianity; they are born again, and the life changer is sent by God in response to human need.

The qualities Spurgeon embodied were never more urgently needed than now. The steady persistence and cheery optimism with which he faced difficulties are examples we cannot neglect. In times of depression, there is real danger of accepting the spirit of defeat. Let us turn to Spurgeon as our guide, following his determination and serenity of spirit.